Gregory Zorzos

The Pythagorean Theory of Music and Color

Gregory Zorzos, a native Hellene, was born in Kallithea, Athens in Greece (Hellas) at 1958. Author and his research work have been distinguished by a lot of official organizations, and Ministries, in Greece and all over the world.
The author has wrote more than 2.800 books, 350 board games, 650 DVDs and 280 cdroms/DVDroms about ancient and modern history in the fields of economics, technical, board games, martial arts, software, love affairs, feasibilities studies, research, case studies, learning languages, Logodynamics, inner research etc.
As a reporter, from his teens, the author has written many articles in many newspapers, magazines etc. and was editor in chief in some of them.
Researches have been approved/accepted from the Ministry of Education, Ministry of Culture, Hellenic Army, Ministry of Foreign Affairs, Unesco (Piraeus and Islands), SAE, etc. Works have been register in Copyright Offices in Greece, USA and Canada.
Many awards and credits around the world.

Gregory Zorzos
P.O. Box 75070, GR-17610 Kallithea, Greece

THE SECRET TEACHINGS OF ALL AGES

by Manly P. Hall

The Pythagorean Theory of Music and Color

Clio Thalia Erato Euterpe Polyhymnia Calliope Terpsichore Urania Melpomene

HARMONY is a state recognized by great philosophers as the immediate prerequisite of beauty. A compound is termed *beautiful* only when its parts are in *harmonious* combination. The world is called beautiful and its Creator is designated the *Good* because good perforce must act in conformity with its own nature; and good acting according to its own nature is harmony, because the good which it accomplishes is harmonious with the good which it is. Beauty, therefore, is harmony manifesting its own intrinsic nature in the world of form.

The universe is made up of successive gradations of good, these gradations ascending from matter (which is the least degree of good) to spirit (which is the greatest degree of good). In man, his superior nature is the *summum bonum.* It therefore follows that his highest nature most readily cognizes good because the good external to him in the world is in harmonic ratio with the good present in his soul. What man terms *evil* is therefore, in common with matter, merely the least degree of its own opposite. The least degree of good presupposes likewise the least degree of harmony and beauty. Thus deformity (evil) is really the least harmonious combination of elements naturally harmonic as individual units. Deformity is unnatural, for, the sum of all things being the *Good*, it is natural that all things should partake of the *Good* and be arranged in combinations that are harmonious. Harmony is the manifesting expression of the *Will* of the eternal *Good*.

THE PHILOSOPHY OF MUSIC

It is highly probable that the Greek initiates gained their knowledge of the philosophic and therapeutic aspects of music from the Egyptians, who, in turn, considered Hermes the founder of the art. According to one legend, this god constructed the first lyre by stretching strings across the concavity of a turtle shell. Both Isis and Osiris were patrons of music and poetry. Plato, in describing the antiquity of these arts among the Egyptians, declared that songs and poetry had existed in Egypt for at least ten thousand years, and that these were of such an exalted and inspiring nature that only gods or godlike men could have composed them. In the Mysteries the lyre was regarded as the secret symbol of the human constitution, the body of the instrument representing the physical form, the strings the nerves, and the musician the spirit. Playing upon the nerves, the spirit thus created the harmonies of normal functioning, which, however, became discords if the nature of man were defiled.

While the early Chinese, Hindus, Persians, Egyptians, Israelites, and Greeks employed both vocal and instrumental music in their religious ceremonials, also to complement their poetry and drama, it remained for Pythagoras to raise the art to its true dignity by demonstrating its mathematical foundation. Although it is said that he himself was not a musician, Pythagoras is now generally credited with the discovery of the diatonic scale. Having first learned the divine theory of music from the priests of the various Mysteries into which he had been accepted, Pythagoras pondered for several years upon the laws governing consonance and dissonance. How he actually solved the problem is unknown, but the following explanation has been invented.

One day while meditating upon the problem of harmony, Pythagoras chanced to pass a brazier's shop where workmen were pounding out a piece of metal upon an anvil. By noting the variances in pitch between the sounds made by large hammers and those made by smaller implements, and carefully estimating the harmonies and discords resulting from combinations of these sounds, he gained his first clue to the musical intervals of the diatonic scale. He entered the shop, and after carefully examining the tools and making mental note of their weights, returned to his own house and constructed an arm of wood so that it: extended out from the wall of his room. At regular intervals along this arm he attached four cords, all of like composition, size, and weight. To the first of these he attached a twelve-pound weight, to the second a nine-pound weight, to the third an eight-pound weight, and to the fourth a six-pound weight. These different weights corresponded to the sizes of the braziers' hammers.

Pythagoras thereupon discovered that the first and fourth strings when sounded together produced the harmonic interval of the octave, for doubling the weight had the same effect as halving the string. The tension of the first string being twice that of the fourth string, their ratio was said to be 2:1, or duple. By similar experimentation he ascertained that the first and third string produced the harmony of the diapente, or the interval of the fifth. The tension of the first string being half again as much as that of the third string, their ratio was said to be 3:2, or sesquialter. Likewise the second and fourth strings, having the same ratio as the first and third strings, yielded a diapente harmony. Continuing his investigation,

Pythagoras discovered that the first and second strings produced the harmony of the diatessaron, or the interval of the third; and the tension of the first string being a third greater than that of the second string, their ratio was said to be 4:3, or sesquitercian. The third and fourth strings, having the same ratio as the first and second strings, produced another harmony of the diatessaron. According to Iamblichus, the second and third strings had the ratio of 8:9, or epogdoan.

The key to harmonic ratios is hidden in the famous Pythagorean tetractys, or pyramid of dots. The *tetractys* is made up of the first four numbers--1, 2, 3, and 4--which in their proportions reveal the intervals of the octave, the diapente, and the diatessaron. While the law of harmonic intervals as set forth above is true, it has been subsequently proved that hammers striking metal in the manner

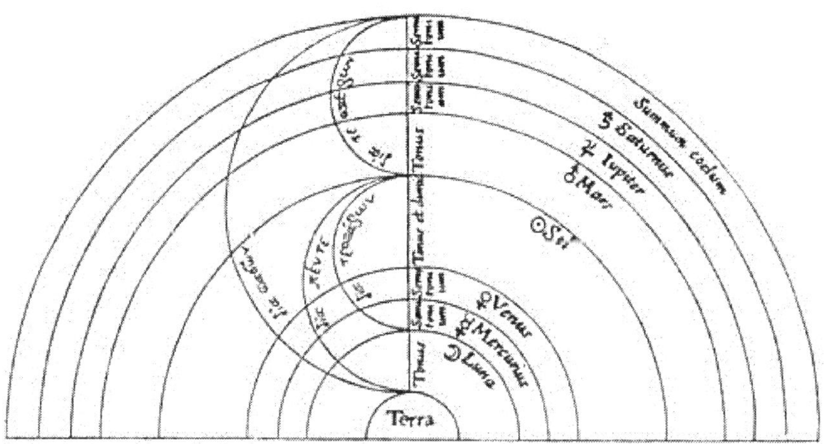

THE INTERVALS AND HARMONIES OF THE SPHERES.

From Stanley's *The History of Philosophy*.

In the Pythagorean concept of the music of the spheres, the interval between the earth and the sphere of the fixed stars was considered to be a diapason--the most perfect harmonic interval. The allowing arrangement is most generally accepted for the musical intervals of the planets between the earth and the sphere of the fixed stars: From the sphere of the earth to the sphere of the moon; one tone; from the sphere of the moon to that of Mercury, one half-tone; from Mercury to Venus, one-half; from Venus to the sun, one and one-half tones; from the sun to Mars, one tone; from Mars to Jupiter, one-half tone; from Jupiter to Saturn, one-half tone; from Saturn to the fixed stars, one-half tone. The sum of these intervals equals the six whole tones of the octave.

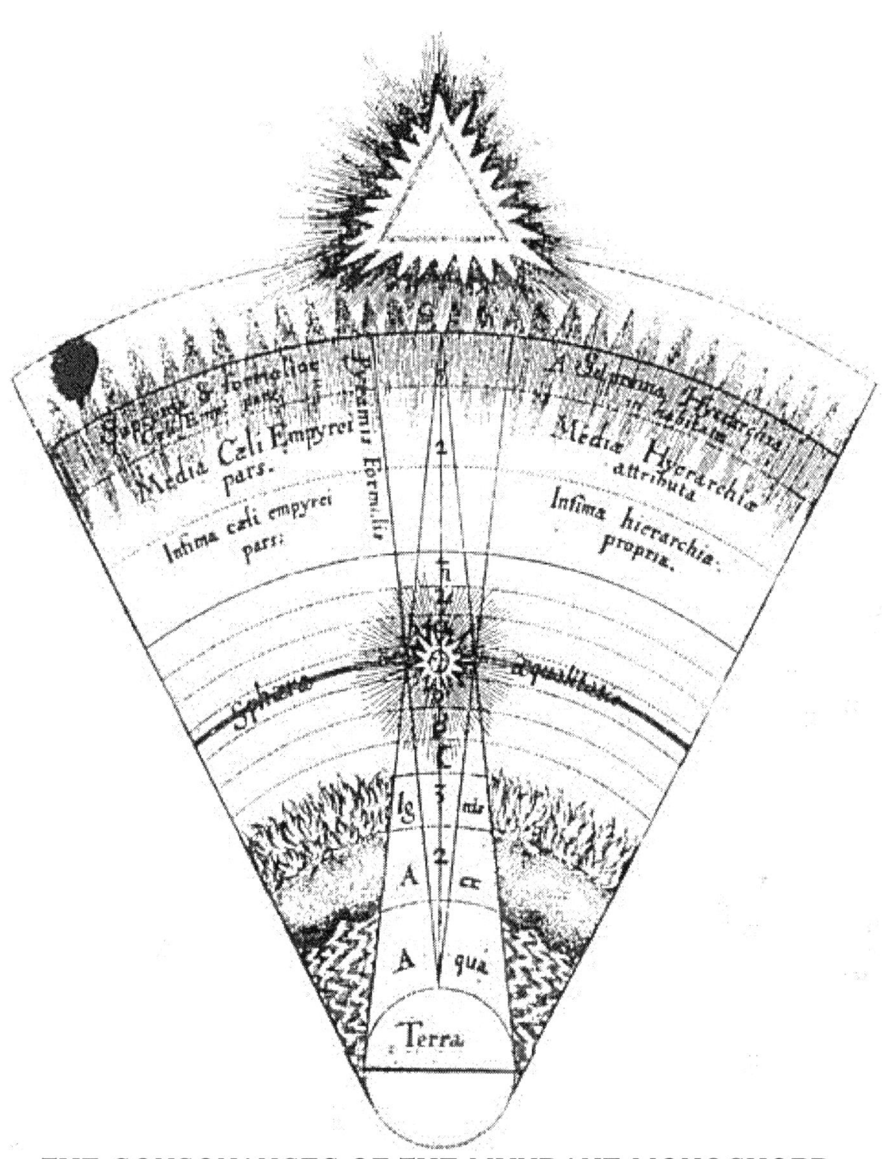

THE CONSONANCES OF THE MUNDANE MONOCHORD.

From Fludd's *De Musica Mundana.*

This diagrammatic sector represents the major gradations of energy and substance between elemental earth and absolute unconditioned force. Beginning with the superior, the fifteen graduated spheres descend in the following order: Limitless and Eternal Life; the superior, the middle, and the inferior Empyrean; the seven planets; and the four elements. Energy is symbolized by Fludd as a pyramid with its base upon the concave surface of the superior Empyrean, and substance as another Pyramid with its base upon the convex surface of the sphere (not planet) of earth. These pyramids demonstrate the relative proportions of energy and substance entering into the composition of the fifteen planes of being. It will be noted that the ascending pyramid of substance touches but does not pierce the fifteenth sphere--that of Limitless and Eternal Life. Likewise, the descending pyramid of energy touches but does not pierce the first sphere--the grossest condition of substance. The plane of the sun is denominated the *sphere of equality*, for here neither energy nor substance predominate. The mundane monochord consists of a hypothetical string stretched from the base of the pyramid of energy to the base of the pyramid of substance.

described will not produce the various tones ascribed to them. In all probability, therefore, Pythagoras actually worked out his theory of harmony from the monochord--a contrivance consisting of a single string stretched between two pegs and supplied with movable frets.

To Pythagoras music was one of the dependencies of the divine science of mathematics, and its harmonies were inflexibly controlled by mathematical proportions. The Pythagoreans averred that mathematics demonstrated the exact method by which the good established and maintained its universe. Number therefore preceded harmony, since it was the immutable law that governs all harmonic proportions. After discovering these harmonic ratios, Pythagoras gradually initiated his disciples into this, the supreme arcanum of his Mysteries. He divided the multitudinous parts of creation into a vast number of planes or spheres, to each of which he assigned a tone, a harmonic interval, a number, a name, a color, and a form. He then proceeded to prove the accuracy of his deductions by demonstrating them upon the different planes of intelligence and substance ranging from the most abstract logical premise to the most concrete geometrical solid. From the common agreement of these diversified methods of proof he established the indisputable existence of certain natural laws.

Having once established music as an exact science, Pythagoras applied his newly found law of harmonic intervals to all the phenomena of Nature, even going so far as to demonstrate the harmonic relationship of the planets, constellations, and elements to each other. A notable example of modern corroboration of ancient philosophical reaching is that of the progression of the elements according to harmonic ratios. While making a list of the elements in the ascending order of their atomic weights, John A. Newlands discovered at every eighth element a distinct repetition of properties. This discovery is known as the *law of octaves* in modern chemistry.

Since they held that harmony must be determined not by the sense perceptions but by reason and mathematics, the Pythagoreans called themselves *Canonics*, as distinguished from musicians of the *Harmonic School*, who asserted taste and instinct to be the true normative principles of harmony. Recognizing, however, the profound effect: of music upon the senses and emotions, Pythagoras did not hesitate to influence the mind and body with what he termed "musical medicine."

Pythagoras evinced such a marked preference for stringed instruments that he even went so far as to warn his disciples against allowing their ears to be defiled by the sounds of flutes or cymbals. He further declared that the soul could be purified from its irrational influences by solemn songs sung to the accompaniment of the lyre. In his investigation of the therapeutic value of harmonics, Pythagoras discovered that the seven modes--or keys--of the Greek system of music had the power to incite or allay the various emotions. It is related that while observing the stars one night he encountered a young man befuddled with strong drink and mad with jealousy who was piling faggots about his mistress' door with the intention of burning the house.

The frenzy of the youth was accentuated by a flutist a short distance away who was playing a tune in the stirring Phrygian mode. Pythagoras induced the musician to change his air to the slow, and rhythmic Spondaic mode, whereupon the intoxicated youth immediately became composed and, gathering up his bundles of wood, returned quietly to his own home.

There is also an account of how Empedocles, a disciple of Pythagoras, by quickly changing the mode of a musical composition he was playing, saved the life of his host, Anchitus, when the latter was threatened with death by the sword of one whose father he had condemned to public execution.

It is also known that Esculapius, the Greek physician, cured sciatica and other diseases of the nerves by blowing a loud trumpet in the presence of the patient.

Pythagoras cured many ailments of the spirit, soul, and body by having certain specially prepared musical compositions played in the presence of the sufferer or by personally reciting short selections from such early poets as Hesiod and Homer.

In his university at Crotona it was customary for the Pythagoreans to open and to close each day with songs--those in the morning calculated to clear the mind from sleep and inspire it to the activities of the coming day; those in the evening of a mode soothing, relaxing, and conducive to rest. At the vernal equinox, Pythagoras caused his disciples to gather in a circle around one of their number who led them in song and played their accompaniment upon a lyre.

The therapeutic music of Pythagoras is described by Iamblichus thus: "And there are certain melodies devised as remedies against the passions of the soul, and also against despondency and lamentation, which Pythagoras invented as things that afford the greatest assistance in these maladies.

And again, he employed other melodies against rage and anger, and against every aberration of the soul. There is also another kind of modulation invented as a remedy against desires." (See *The Life of Pythagoras.*)

It is probable that the Pythagoreans recognized a connection between the seven Greek modes and the planets. As an example, Pliny declares that Saturn moves in the Dorian mode and Jupiter in the Phrygian mode. It is also apparent that the temperaments are keyed to the various modes, and the passions likewise. Thus, anger--which is a fiery passion--may be accentuated by a fiery mode or its power neutralized by a watery mode.

The far-reaching effect exercised by music upon the culture of the Greeks is thus summed up by Emil Nauman: "Plato depreciated the notion that music was intended solely to create cheerful and agreeable emotions, maintaining rather that it should inculcate a love of all that is noble, and hatred of all that is mean, and that nothing could more strongly influence man's innermost feelings than melody and rhythm.

Firmly convinced of this, he agreed with Damon of Athens, the musical instructor of Socrates, that the introduction of a new and presumably enervating scale would endanger the future of a whole nation, and that it was not possible to alter a key without shaking the very foundations of the State.

Plato affirmed that music which ennobled the mind was of a far higher kind than that which merely appealed to the senses, and he strongly insisted that it was the paramount duty of the Legislature to suppress all music of an effeminate and lascivious character, and to encourage only s that which was pure and dignified; that bold and stirring melodies were for men, gentle and soothing ones for women.

From this it is evident that music played a considerable part in the education of the Greek youth. The greatest care was also to be taken in the selection of instrumental music, because the absence of words rendered its signification doubtful, and it was difficult to foresee whether it would exercise upon the people a benign or baneful influence.

Popular taste, being always tickled by sensuous and meretricious effects, was to be treated with deserved contempt. (See *The History of Music.*)

Even today martial music is used with telling effect in times of war, and religious music, while no longer developed in accordance with the ancient theory, still profoundly influences the emotions of the laity.

THE MUSIC OF THE SPHERES

The most sublime but least known of all the Pythagorean speculations was that of sidereal harmonics.

It was said that of all men only Pythagoras heard *the music of the spheres.* Apparently the Chaldeans were the first people to conceive of the heavenly bodies joining in a cosmic chant as they moved in stately manner across the sky.

Job describes a time "when the stars of the morning sang together," and in *The Merchant of Venice* the author of the Shakesperian plays

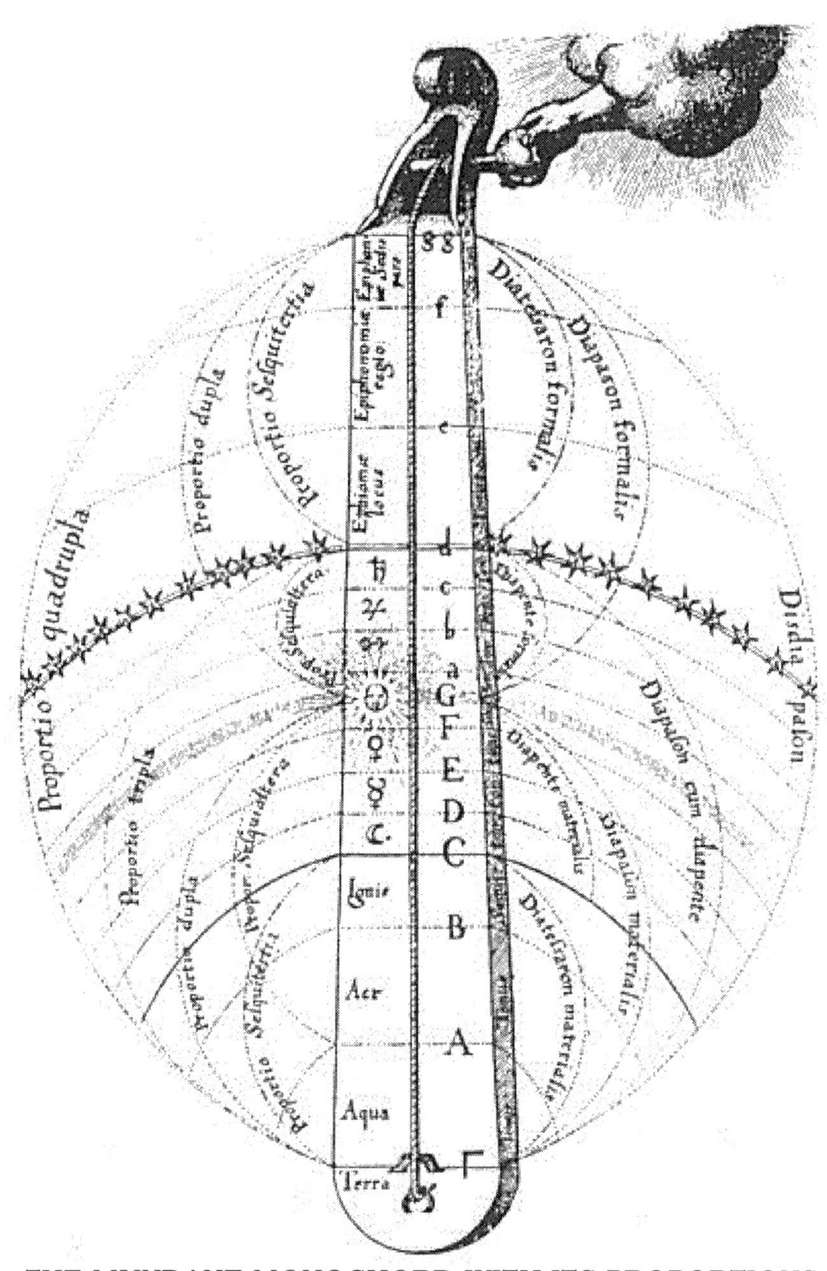

THE MUNDANE MONOCHORD WITH ITS PROPORTIONS AND INTERVALS.

From Fludd's *De Musica Mundana.*

In this chart is set forth a summary of Fludd's theory of universal music. The interval between the element of earth and the highest heaven is considered as a double octave, thus showing the two extremes of existence to be in disdiapason harmony.

It is signifies that the highest heaven, the sun, and the earth have the same time, the difference being in pitch. The sun is the lower octave of the highest heaven and the earth the lower octave of the sun.

The lower octave (to G) comprises that part of the universe in which substance predominate over energy. Its harmonies, therefore, are more gross than those of the higher octave (G to g) wherein energy predominates over substance.

"If struck in the more spiritual part," writes Fludd, "the monochord will give eternal life; if in the more material part, transitory life." It will be noted that certain elements, planets, and celestial spheres sustain a harmonic ratio to each other, Fludd advanced this as a key to the sympathies and antipathies existing between the various departments of Nature.

writes: "There's not the smallest orb which thou behold'st but in his motion like an angel sings." So little remains, however, of the Pythagorean system of celestial music that it is only possible to approximate his actual theory.

Pythagoras conceived the universe to be an immense monochord, with its single string connected at its upper end to absolute spirit and at its lower end to absolute matter--in other words, a cord stretched between heaven and earth.

Counting inward from the circumference of the heavens, Pythagoras, according to some authorities, divided the universe into nine parts; according to others, into twelve parts.

The twelvefold system was as follows: The first division was called the *empyrean*, or the sphere of the fixed stars, and was the dwelling place of the immortals. The second to twelfth divisions were (in order) the spheres of Saturn, Jupiter, Mars, the sun, Venus, Mercury, and the moon, and fire, air, water, and earth. This arrangement of the seven planets (the sun and moon being regarded as planets in the old astronomy) is identical with the candlestick symbolism of the Jews--the sun in the center as the main stem with three planets on either side of it.

The names given by the Pythagoreans to the various notes of the diatonic scale were, according to Macrobius, derived from an estimation of the velocity and magnitude of the planetary bodies. Each of these gigantic spheres as it rushed endlessly through space was believed to sound a certain tone caused by its continuous displacement of the *thereal diffusion.*

As these tones were a manifestation of divine order and motion, it must necessarily follow that they partook of the harmony of their own source. "The assertion that the planets in their revolutions round the earth uttered certain sounds differing according to their respective 'magnitude, celerity and local distance,' was commonly made by the Greeks. Thus Saturn, the farthest planet, was said to give the gravest note, while the Moon, which is the nearest, gave the sharpest.

'These sounds of the seven planets, and the sphere of the fixed stars, together with that above us [Antichthon], are the nine Muses, and their joint symphony is called Mnemosyne.'" (See *The Canon.*)

This quotation contains an obscure reference to the ninefold division of the universe previously mentioned.

The Greek initiates also recognized a fundamental relationship between the individual heavens or spheres of the seven planets, and the seven sacred vowels.

The first heaven uttered the sound of the sacred vowel A (Alpha); the second heaven, the sacred vowel E (Epsilon); the third, H (Eta); the fourth, I (Iota); the fifth, O (Omicron); the sixth, Y (Upsilon); and the seventh heaven, the sacred vowel (Omega).

When these seven heavens sing together they produce a perfect harmony which ascends as an everlasting praise to the throne of the Creator. (See Iren us' *Against Heresies.*)

Although not so stated, it is probable that the planetary heavens are to be considered as ascending in the Pythagorean order, beginning with the sphere of the moon, which would be the first heaven.

Many early instruments had seven Strings, and it is generally conceded that Pythagoras was the one who added the eighth string to the lyre of Terpander.

The seven strings were always related both to their correspondences in the human body and to the planets. The names of God were also conceived to be formed from combinations of the seven planetary harmonies.

The Egyptians confined their sacred songs to the seven primary sounds, forbidding any others to be uttered in their temples. One of their hymns contained the following invocation: "The seven sounding tones praise Thee, the Great God, the ceaseless working Father of the whole universe."

In another the Deity describe
thus: "I am the great indestructi
the whole world, attuning the sc
heavens. (See Nauman's *I*
Music.)

The Pythagoreans believed that everything which existed had a voice and that all creatures were eternally singing the praise of the Creator.

Man fails to hear these divine melodies because his soul is enmeshed in the illusion of material existence. When he liberates himself from the bondage of the lower world with its sense limitations, *the music of the spheres* will again be audible as it was in the Golden Age.

Harmony recognizes harmony, and when the human soul regains its true estate it will not only hear the celestial choir but also join with it in an everlasting anthem of praise to that Eternal *Good* controlling the infinite number of parts and conditions of Being.

The Greek Mysteries included in their doctrines a magnificent concept of the relationship existing between music and form.

The elements of architecture, for example, were considered as comparable to musical modes and notes, or as having a musical counterpart.

Consequently when a building was erected in which a number of these elements were combined, the structure was then likened to a musical chord, which was harmonic only when it fully satisfied the mathematical requirements of harmonic intervals.

The realization of this analogy between sound and form led Goethe to declare that "architecture is crystallized music."

In constructing their temples of initiation, the early priests frequently demonstrated their superior knowledge of the principles underlying the phenomena known as vibration.

A considerable part of the Mystery rituals consisted of invocations and intonements, for which purpose special sound chambers were constructed.

A word whispered in one of these apartments was so intensified that the reverberations made the entire building sway and be filled with a deafening roar.

The very wood and stone used in the erection of these sacred buildings eventually became so thoroughly permeated with the sound vibrations of the religious ceremonies that when struck they would reproduce the same tones thus repeatedly impressed into their substances by the rituals.

Every element in Nature has its individual keynote. If these elements are combined in a composite structure the result is a chord that, if sounded, will disintegrate the compound into its integral parts.

Likewise each individual has a keynote that, if sounded, will destroy him. The allegory of the walls of Jericho falling when the trumpets of Israel were sounded is undoubtedly intended to set forth the arcane significance of individual keynote or vibration.

THE PHILOSOPHY OF COLOR

"Light," writes Edwin D. Babbitt, "reveals the glories of the external world and yet is the most glorious of them all. It gives beauty, reveals beauty and is itself most beautiful.

It is the analyzer, the truth-teller and the exposer of shams, for it shows things as they are. Its infinite streams measure off the universe and flow into our telescopes from stars which are quintillions of miles distant.

On the other hand it descends to objects inconceivably small, and reveals through the microscope objects fifty millions of times less than can be seen by the naked eye. Like all other fine forces, its movement is wonderfully soft, yet penetrating and powerful.

its vivifying influence, vegetable, ınd human life must immediately om the earth, and general ruin e.

We shall do well, then, to consider this potential and beautiful principle of light and its component colors, for the more deeply we penetrate into its inner laws, the more will it present itself as a marvelous storehouse of power to vitalize, heal, refine, and delight mankind." (See *The Principles of Light and Color.*)

Since light is the basic physical manifestation of life, bathing all creation in its radiance, it is highly important to realize, in part at least, the subtle nature of this divine substance.

That which is called *light* is actually a rate of vibration causing certain reactions upon the optic nerve. Few realize how they are walled in by the limitations

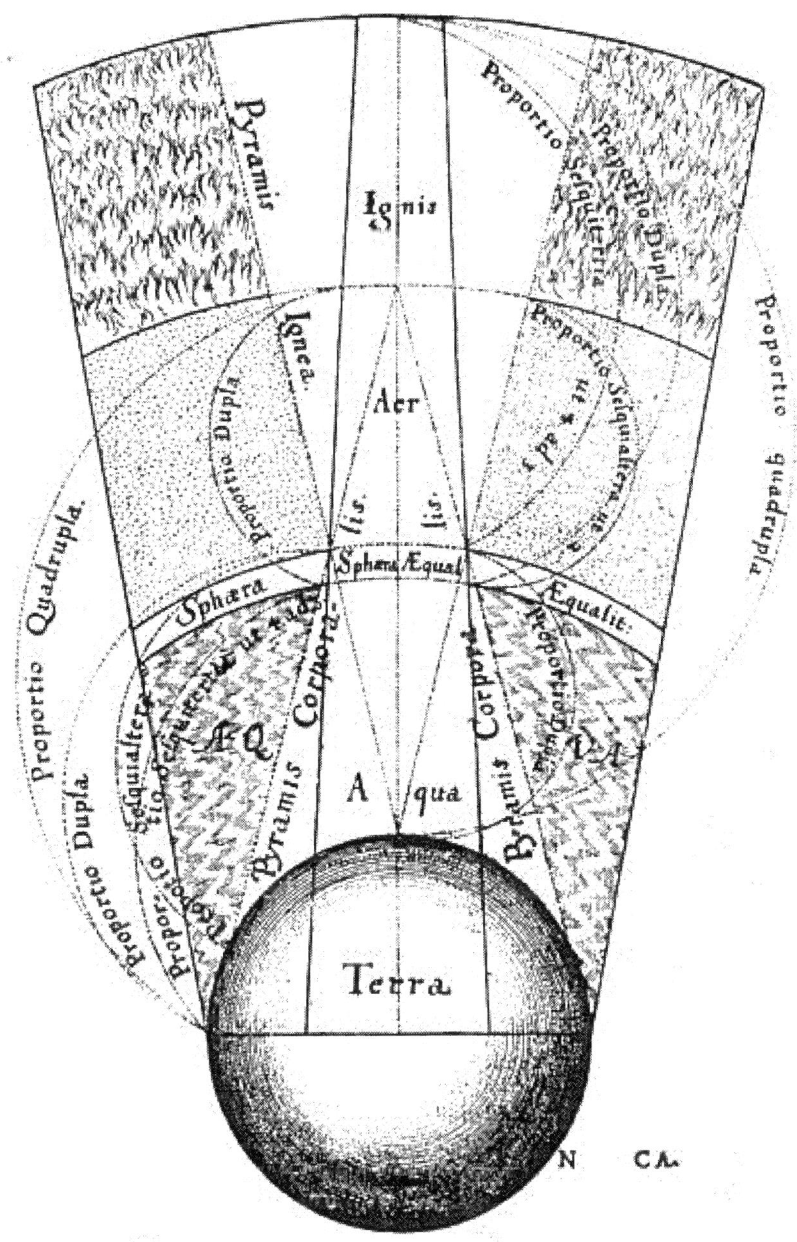

THE THEORY OF ELEMENTAL MUSIC.

From Fludd's *De Musica Mundana.*

In this diagram two interpenetrating pyramids are again employed, one of which represents fire and the other earth.

It is demonstrated according to the law of elemental harmony that fire does not enter into the composition of earth nor earth into the composition of fire.

The figures on the chart disclose the harmonic relationships existing between the four primary elements according to both Fludd and the Pythagoreans.

Earth consists of four parts of its own nature; water of three parts of earth and one part of fire. The sphere of equality is a hypothetical point where there is an equilibrium of two parts of earth and two parts of fire.

Air is composed of three parts of fire and one part of earth; fire, of four parts of its own nature.

Thus earth and water bear to each other the ratio of 4 to 3, or the diatessaron harmony, and water and the sphere of equality the ratio of 3 to 2, or the diapente harmony.

Fire and air also bear to each other the ratio of 4 to 3, or the diatessaron harmony, and air and the sphere of equality the ratio of 3 to 2, or the diapente harmony.

As the sum of a diatessaron and a diapente equals a diapason, or octave, it is evident that both the sphere of fire and the sphere of earth are in diapason harmony with the sphere of equality, and also that fire and earth are in disdiapason harmony with each other.

of the sense perceptions. 'Not only is there a great deal more to light than anyone has ever seen but there are also unknown forms of light which no optical equipment will ever register.

There are unnumbered colors which cannot be seen, as well as sounds which cannot be heard, odors which cannot be smelt, flavors which cannot be tasted, and substances which cannot be felt.

Man is thus surrounded by a supersensible universe of which he knows nothing because the centers of sense perception within himself have not been developed sufficiently to respond to the subtler rates of vibration of which that universe is composed.

Among both civilized and savage peoples color has been accepted as a natural language in which to couch their religious and philosophical doctrines.

The ancient city of Ecbatana as described by Herodotus, its seven walls colored according to the seven planets, revealed the knowledge of this subject possessed by the Persian Magi.

The famous *zikkurat* or astronomical tower of the god Nebo at Borsippa ascended in seven great steps or stages, each step being painted in the key color of one of the planetary bodies. (See Lenormant's *Chaldean Magic.*)

It is thus evident that the Babylonians were familiar with the concept of the spectrum in its relation to the seven Creative Gods or Powers. In India, one of the Mogul emperors caused a fountain to be made with seven levels.

The water pouring down the sides through specially arranged channels changed color as it descended, passing sequentially through all shades of the spectrum.

In Tibet, color is employed by the native artists to express various moods. L. Austine Waddell, writing of Northern Buddhist art, notes that in Tibetan mythology "White and yellow complexions usually typify mild moods, while the red, blue, and black belong to fierce forms, though sometimes light blue, as indicating the sky, means merely celestial.

Generally the gods are pictured white, goblins red, and devils black, like their European relative." (See *The Buddhism of Tibet.*)

In *Meno*, Plato, speaking through Socrates, describes color as "an effluence of form, commensurate with sight, and sensible."

In *The tetus* he discourses more at length on the subject thus: "Let us carry out the principle which has just been affirmed, that nothing is self-existent, and then we shall see that every color, white, black, and every other color, arises out of the eye meeting the appropriate motion, and that what we term the substance of each color is neither the active nor the passive element, but something which passes between them, and is peculiar to each percipient; are you certain that the several colors appear to every animal--say a dog--as they appear to you?"

In the Pythagorean *tetractys*--the supreme symbol of universal forces and processes--are set forth the theories of the Greeks concerning color and music.

The first three dots represent the threefold White Light, which is the Godhead containing potentially all sound and color. The remaining seven dots are the colors of the spectrum and the notes of the musical scale.

The colors and tones are the active creative powers which, emanating from the First Cause, establish the universe.

The seven are divided into two groups, one containing three powers and the other four a relationship also shown in the *tetractys.*

The higher group--that of three--becomes the spiritual nature of the created universe; the lower group--that of four--manifests as the irrational sphere, or inferior world.

In the Mysteries the seven *Logi*, or Creative Lords, are shown as streams of force issuing from the mouth of the Eternal One. This signifies the spectrum being extracted from the white light of the Supreme Deity.

The seven Creators, or Fabricators, of the inferior spheres were called by the Jews the *Elohim*. By the Egyptians they were referred to as the *Builders* (sometimes as the *Governors*) and are depicted with great knives in their hands with which they carved the universe from its primordial substance.

Worship of the planets is based upon their acceptation as the cosmic embodiments of the seven creative attributes of God.

The Lords of the planets were described as dwelling within the body of the sun, for the true nature of the sun, being analogous to the white light, contains the seeds of all the tone and color potencies which it manifests.

There are numerous arbitrary arrangements setting forth the mutual relationships of the planets, the colors, and the musical notes. The most satisfactory system is that based upon the *law of the octave.*

The sense of hearing has a much wider scope than that of sight, for whereas the ear can register from nine to eleven octaves of sound the eye is restricted to the cognition of but seven fundamental color tones, or one tone short of the octave. Red, when posited as the lowest color tone in the scale of chromatics, thus corresponds to *do*, the first note of the musical scale.

[illegible]ng the analogy, orange [illegible]nds to *re*, yellow to *mi*, green to [illegible] *sol*, indigo to *la*, and violet to *si* [illegible] eighth color tone necessary to [illegible] the scale should be the higher octave of red, the first color tone.

The accuracy of the above arrangement is attested by two striking facts: (1) the three fundamental notes of the musical scale--the first, the third, and the fifth--correspond with the three primary colors--red, yellow, and blue; (2) the seventh, and least perfect, note of the musical scale corresponds with purple, the least perfect tone of the color scale.

In *The Principles of Light and Color*, Edwin D. Babbitt confirms the correspondence of the color and musical scales: "As C is at the bottom of the musical scale and made with the coarsest waves of air, so is red at the bottom of the chromatic scale and made with the coarsest waves of luminous ether.

As the musical note B [the seventh note of the scale] requires 45 vibrations of air every time the note C at the lower end of the scale requires 24, or but little over half as many, so does extreme violet require about 300 trillions of vibrations of ether in a second, while extreme red requires only about 450 trillions, which also are but little more than half as many.

When one musical octave is finished another one commences and progresses with just twice as many vibrations as were used in the first octave, and so the same notes are repeated on a finer scale.

In the same way when the scale of colors visible to the ordinary eye is completed in the violet, another octave of finer invisible colors, with just twice as many vibrations, will commence and progress on precisely the same law."

hen the colors are related to the twelve is of the zodiac, they are arranged as the spokes of a wheel.

To Aries is assigned pure red; to Taurus, red-orange; to Gemini, pure orange; to Cancer, orange-yellow; to Leo, pure yellow; to Virgo, yellow-green; to Libra, pure green; to Scorpio, green-blue; to Sagittarius, pure blue; to Capricorn, blue-violet; to Aquarius, pure violet; and to Pisces, violet-red.

In expounding the Eastern system of esoteric philosophy, H. P. Blavatsky relates the colors to the septenary constitution of man and the seven states of matter as follows:

COLOR	PRINCIPLES OF MAN	STATES OF MATTER
Violet	*Chaya*, or Etheric Double	Ether
Indigo	Higher *Manas*, or Spiritual Intelligence	Critical State called
Blue	Auric Envelope	Steam or Vapor
Green	Lower *Manas*, or Animal Soul	Critical State
Yellow	*Buddhi*, or Spiritual Soul	Water
Orange	*Prana*, or Life Principle	Critical State
Red	*Kama Rupa*, or Seat of Animal Life	Ice

This arrangement of the colors of the spectrum and the musical notes of the octave necessitates a different grouping of the planets in order to preserve their proper tone and color analogies.

Thus *do* becomes Mars; *re*, the sun; *mi*, Mercury; *fa*, Saturn; *sol*, Jupiter; *la*, Venus; *si* (*ti*) the moon. (See *The E. S. Instructions*.)

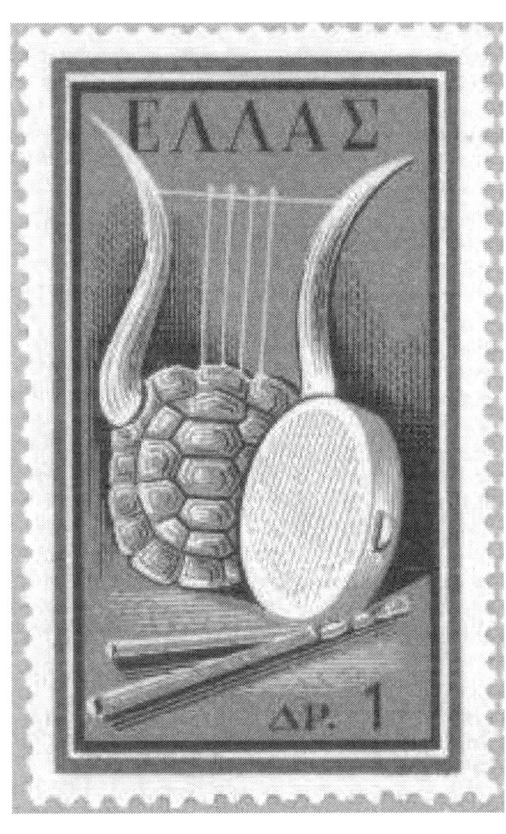

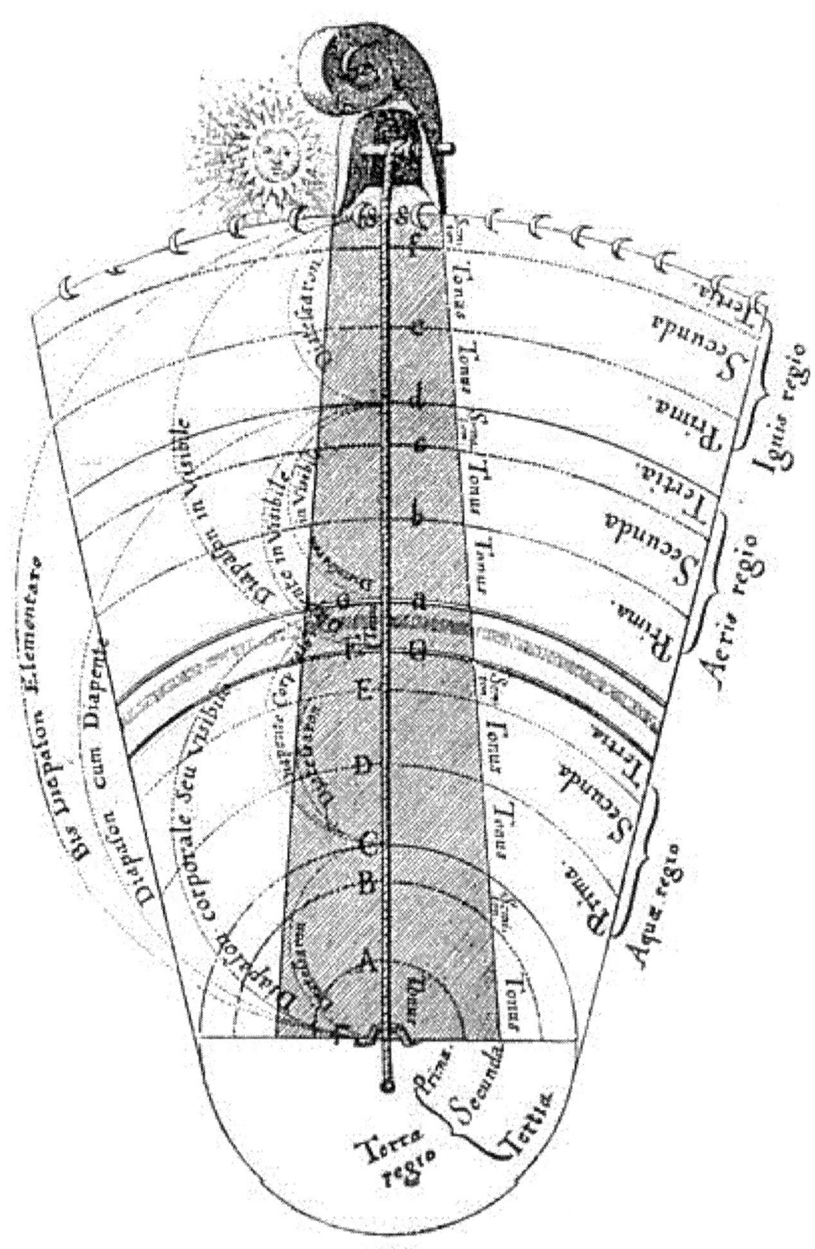

THE FOUR ELEMENTS AND THEIR CONSONANTAL INTERVALS.

From Fludd's *De Musica Mundana.*

In this diagram Fludd has divided each of the four Primary elements into three subdivisions. The first division of each element is the grossest, partaking somewhat of the substance directly inferior to itself (except in the case of the earth, which has no state inferior to itself).

The second division consists of the element in its relatively pure state, while the third division is that condition wherein the element partakes somewhat of the substance immediately superior to itself.

For example the lowest division of the element of water is sedimentary, as it contains earth substance in solution; the second division represents water in its most common state--salty--as in the case of the ocean; and the third division is water in its purest state--free from salt.

The harmonic interval assigned to the lowest division of each element is one tone, to the central division also a tone, but to the higher division a half-tone because it partakes of the division immediately above it. Fludd emphasizes the fact that as the elements ascend in series of two and a half tones, the diatessaron is the dominating harmonic interval of the elements.

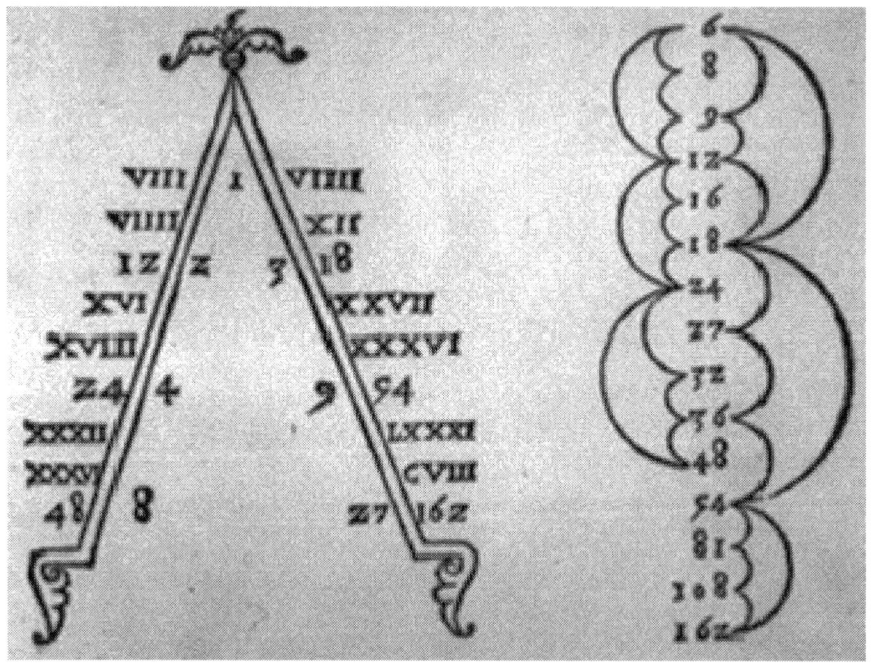

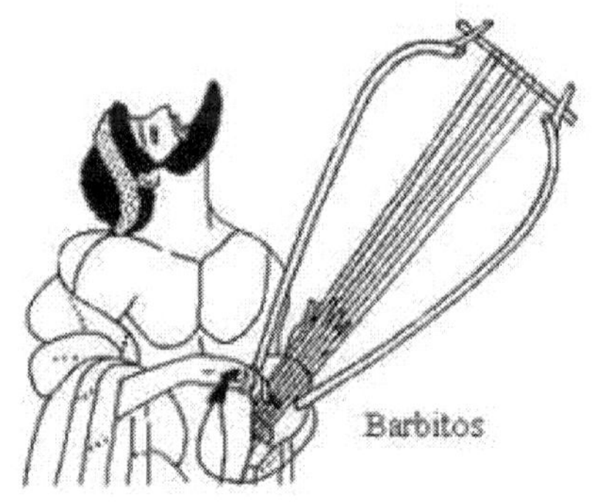

Diuersarum uolucrium voces
notis musicis expressæ
Gallicinium
Cuculicu Cuculicu Cuculicu
A
Vox parturientis Gallinæ
to to to to to to to to to to to to to to to to to to
B
glo glo glo
C
Vox Cuculi
Gucu gucu gucu gucu
E
Vox Coturnicis
Bikebik bikebik bikebik
D

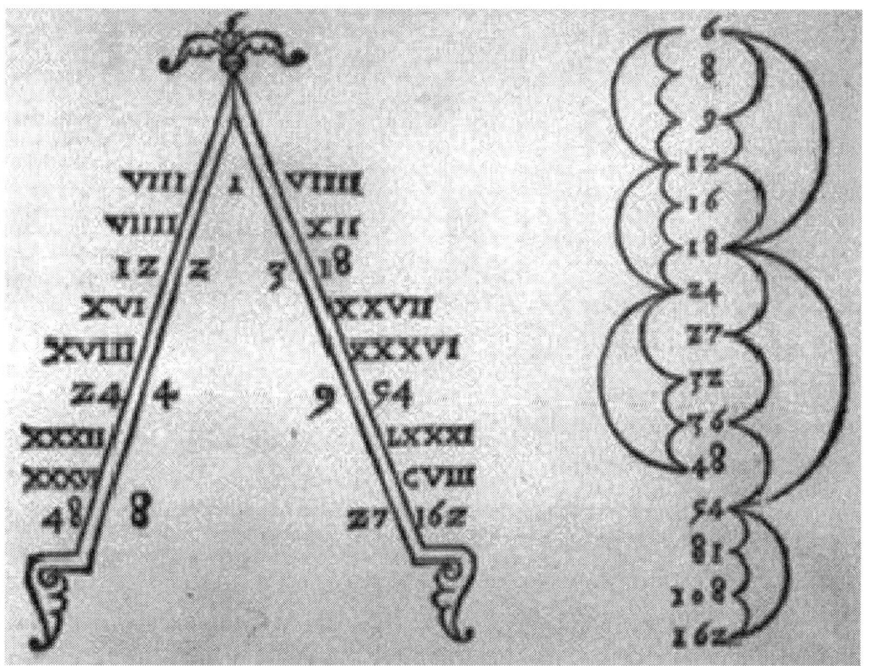
VIII 1 VIIII
VIIII XII
12 2 3 18
XVI XXVII
XVIII XXXVI
24 4 9 54
XXXII LXXXI
XXXVI CVIII
48 8 27 162
6
8
9
12
16
18
24
27
32
36
48
54
81
108
162

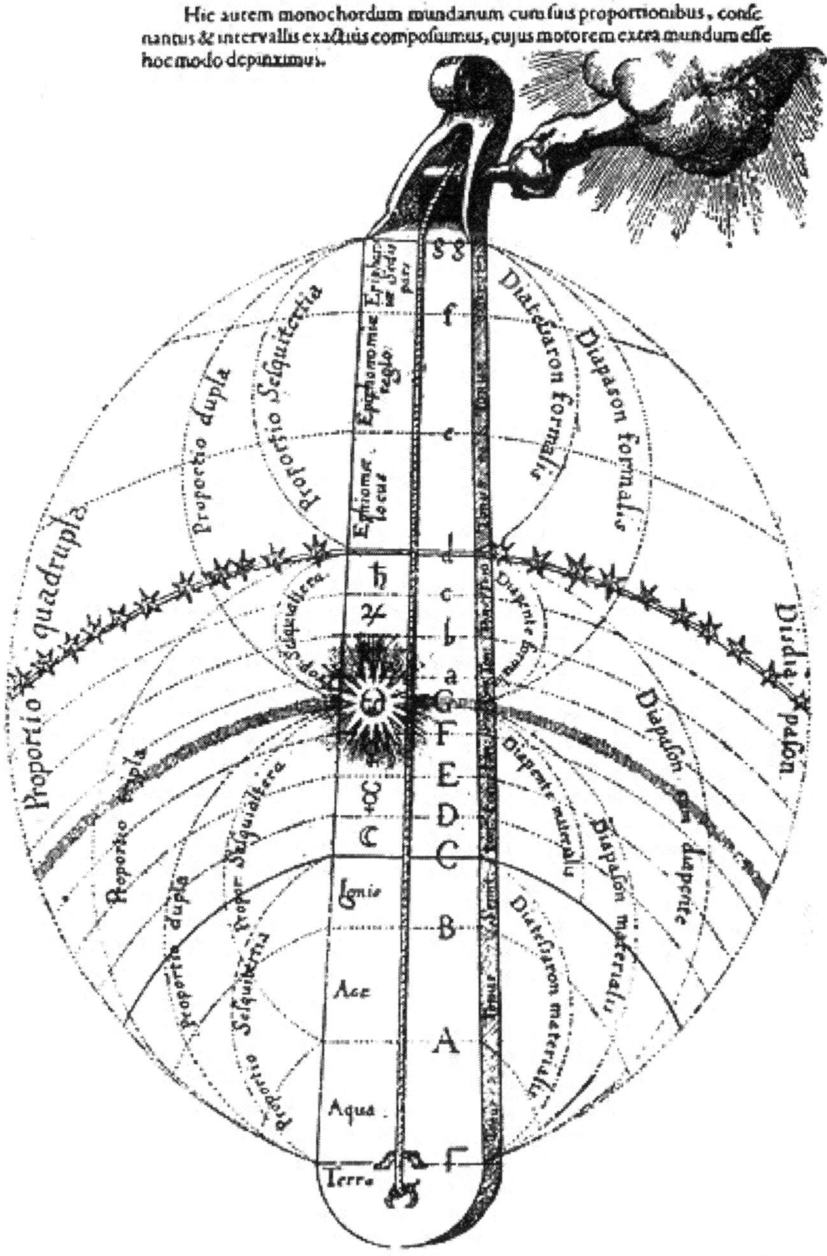
Hic autem monochordum mundanum cum suis proportionibus, conso-
nantus & intervallis exactis composuimus, cujus motorem extra mundum esse
hoc modo depinximus.
Proportio quadrupla
Proportio dupla
Proportio Sesquitertia
Diatessaron formalis
Diapason formalis
Disdiapason
Proportio Sesquialtera
Diapason cum diapente
Diapente materialis
Diapason materialis
Diatessaron materialis
Proportio dupla
Proportio Sesquitertia
Empyreum
Ethereum
Ignis
Aer
Aqua
Terra
gg
f
e
d
c
b
a
G
F
E
D
C
B
A
Γ

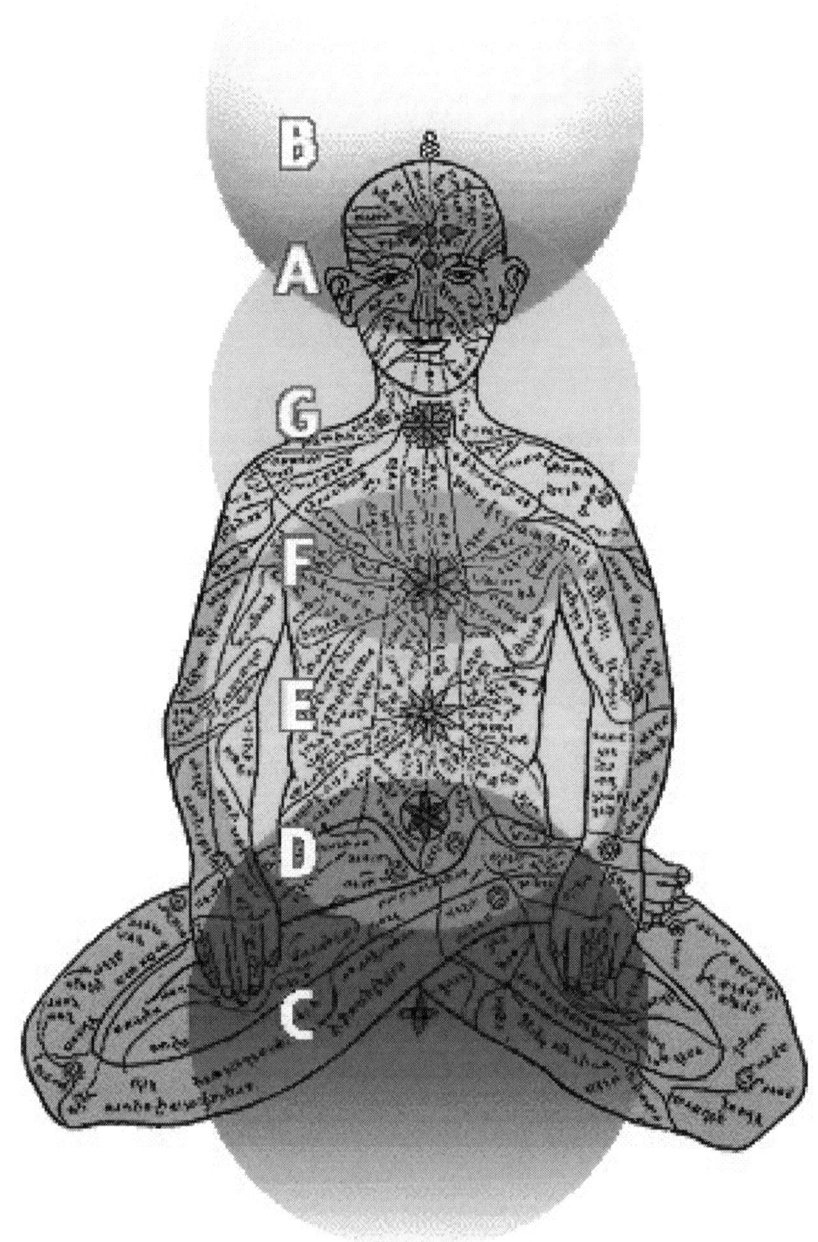
B
A
G
F
E
D
C

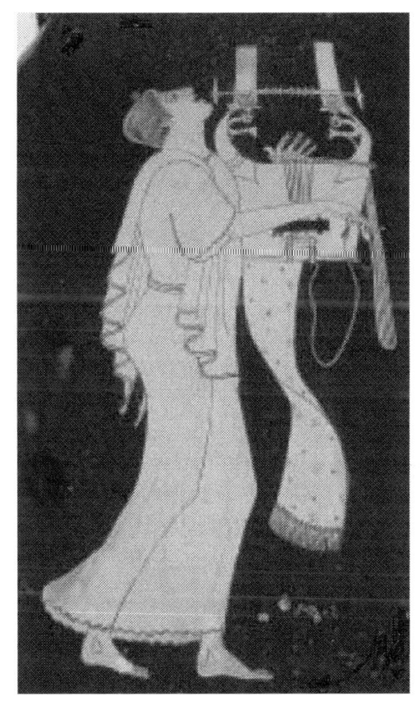

List of All Major Scales with Notes, Diatonic Triads, & Relative Minors

C Major Scale
Notes: C – D – E – F – G – A – B
Diatonic Triads: CM – Dm – Em – FM – GM – Am – Bdim
Relative Minor: A minor

G Major Scale

Notes: G – A – B – C – D – E – F#
Diatonic Triads: GM – Am – Bm – CM – DM – Em – F#dim
Relative Minor: E minor

D Major Scale

Notes: D – E – F# – G – A – B – C#
Diatonic Triads: DM – Em – F#m – G – A – Bb – C#dim
Relative Minor: B minor

A Major Scale

Notes: A – B – C# – D – E – F# – G#
Diatonic Triads: AM – Bm – C#m – DM – EM – F#m – G#dim
Relative Minor: F# minor

E Major Scale

Notes: E – F# – G# – A – B – C# – D#
Diatonic Triads: EM – F#m – G#m – AM – BM – C#m – D#dim
Relative Minor: C# minor

B Major Scale

Notes: B – C# – D# – E – F# – G# – A#
Diatonic Triads: BM – C#m – D#m – EM – F#M – G#m – A#dim
Relative Minor: G# minor

F# Major Scale

Notes: F# – G# – A# – B – C# – D# – E#
Diatonic Triads: F#M – G#m – A#m – BM – C#M – D#m – E#dim
Relative Minor: D# minor

Db Major Scale

Notes: Db – Eb – F – Gb – Ab – Bb – C
Diatonic Triads: DbM – Ebm – Fm – GbM – AbM – Bbm – Cdim
Relative Minor: Bb minor

Ab Major Scale

Notes: Ab – Bb – C – Db – Eb – F – G
Diatonic Triads: AbM – Bbm – Cm – DbM – EbM – Fm – Gdim
Relative Minor: F minor

Eb Major Scale

Notes: Eb – F – G – Ab – Bb – C – D
Diatonic Triads: EbM – Fm – Gm – AbM – BbM – Cm – Ddim
Relative Minor: C minor

Bb Major Scale

Notes: Bb – C – D – Eb – F – G – A
Diatonic Triads: BbM – Cm – Dm – Eb – F – Gm – Adim
Relative Minor: G minor

F Major Scale

Notes: F – G – A – Bb – C – D – E
Diatonic Triads: FM – Gm – Am – BbM – CM – Dm – Edim
Relative Minor: D minor

Major

Cb	Cb Db Eb Fb Gb Ab Bb Cb
Gb	Gb Ab Bb C Db Eb F Gb
Db	Db Eb F Gb Ab Bb C Db
Ab	Ab Bb C Db Eb F G Ab
Eb	Es F G Ab Bb C D Eb
Bb	Bb C D Eb F G A Bb
F	F G A Bb C D E F
C	C D E F G A B C
G	G A B C D E F# G
D	D E F# G A B C# D
A	A B C# D E F# G# A
E	E F# G# A B C# D# E
B	B C# D# E F# G# A# B
F#	F# G# A# B C# D# E# F#
C#	C# D# E# F# G# A# B# C#

Melodic Minor

Cb	Ab Bb Cb Db Eb F G Ab
Gb	Eb F Gb Ab Bb C D Eb
Db	Bb C Db Eb F G A Bb
Ab	F G Ab Bb C D E F
Eb	C D Eb F G A B C
Bb	G A Bb C D E F# G
F	D E F G A B C# D
C	A B C D E F# G# A
G	E F# G A B C# D# E
D	B C# D E F# G# A# B
A	F# G# A B C# D# E# F#
E	C# D# E F# G# A# B# C#
B	G# A# B C# D# E# Fx G#
F#	D# E# F# G# A# B# Cx D#
C#	A# B# C# D# E# Fx Gx A#

Harmonic Minor

Cb Ab Bb Cb Db Eb Fb G Ab

Gb Eb F Gb Ab Bb Cb D Eb

Db Bb C Db Eb F Gb A Bb

Ab F G Ab Bb C Db E F

Eb C D Eb F G Ab B C

Bb G A Bb C D Eb F# G

F D E F G A Bb C# D

C A B C D E F G# A

G E F# G A B C D# E

D B C# D E F# G A# B

A F# G# A B C# D E# F#

E C# D# E F# G# A B# C#

B G# A# B C# D# E Fx G#

F# D# E# F# G# A# B Cx D#

C# A# B# C# D# F# Gx A#

Natural Minor

Cb Ab Bb Cb Db Eb Fb Gb Ab

Gb Eb F Gb Ab Bb Cb Db Eb

Db Bb C Db Eb F Gb Ab Bb

Ab F G Ab Bb C Db Eb F

Eb C D Eb F G Ab Bb C

Bb G A Bb C D Eb F G

F D E F G A Bb C D

C A B C D E F G A

G E F# G A B C D E

D B C# D E F# G A B

A F# G# A B C# D E F#

E C# D# E F# G# A B C#

B G # A# B C# D# E F# G#

F# D# E# F# G# A# B C# D#

C# A# B# C# D# E# F# G# A#

medieval church modes

mode I	Dorian	**D**, E, F, G, A, B, C, **D** - - finalis is D
mode II	Hypodorian	A, B, C, **D**, E, F, G, A - - finalis is D
mode III	Phrygian (fridg'-ian)	**E**, F, G, A, B, C, D, **E** - - finalis is E
mode IV	Hypophrygian	B, C, D, **E**, F, G, A, B - - finalis is E
mode V	Lydian	**F**, G, A, B, C, D, E, **F** - - finalis is F
mode VI	Hypolydian	C, D, E, **F**, G, A, B, C - - finalis is F
mode VII	Mixolydian	**G**, A, B, C, D, E, F, **G** - - finalis is G
mode VIII	Hypomixolydian	D, E, F, **G**, A, B, C, D - - finalis is G

In the 16th century, the eight-mode system of the Gregorian

mode IX	Aeolian	**A**, B, C, D, E, F, G, **A** - - finalis is A
mode X	Hypoaeolian	E, F, G, **A**, B, C, D, E - - finalis is A
mode XI	Ionian	**C**, D, E, F, G, A, B, **C** - - finalis is C
mode XII	Hypoionian	G, A, B, **C**, D, E, F, G - - finalis is C

Did you catch that the medieval & middle ages musicians

mode XIII	Locrian	**B**, C, D, E, F, G, A, **B** - - finalis is B
mode XIV	Hypolocrian	F, G, A, **B**, C, D, E, F - - finalis is B

authentic modes or:

Ionian (major)	C, D, E, F, G, A, B, C
Dorian	D, E, F, G, A, B, C, D
Phrygian	E, F, G, A, B, C, D, E
Lydian	F, G, A, B, C, D, E, F
Mixolydian	G, A, B, C, D, E, F, G
Aeolian (minor)	A, B, C, D, E, F, G, A
Locrian	B, D, C, E, F, G, A, B

Greek Esoteric Music Theory

The Elemental Tetrachord

Vowels	Epsilon (ay)	Alpha (ah)	Eta (eh)	Omega (aw)
Primary pitches	A	B	C	D
Secondary pitches	a	E	F	G
Elements	Earth	Water	Air	Fire
Qualities	Dry	Cool	Moist	Warm
Seasons	Autumn	Winter	Spring	Summer
Directions	West	North	East	South
Deities	Hera Demeter	Persephone Aphrodite	Zeus Dionysos	Hades Hephaistos

Greek Esoteric Music Theory

The Four-String Lyre of Hermes

Musical Tetractys	Fixed Note	Element	Humor	Quality	Season	Moon Phase
6	e Nêtê	Fire	Yellow Bile (Choler.)	Warm	Summer	to Full
8	b Paramesê	Air	Blood (Sang.)	Moist	Spring	to 1st Q
9	a Mesê	Water	Phlegm (Phleg.)	Cool	Winter	to New
12	E Hypatê	Earth	Black Bile (Melan.)	Dry	Autumn	to 3rd Q

METRE AND RHYTHMS

\- = long syllable
u = short syllable
macron and breve notation

Disyllables

u u Pyrrhus-Dibrach
u - Iamb
\- u Trochee-Choree (Choreus)
\- - Spondee

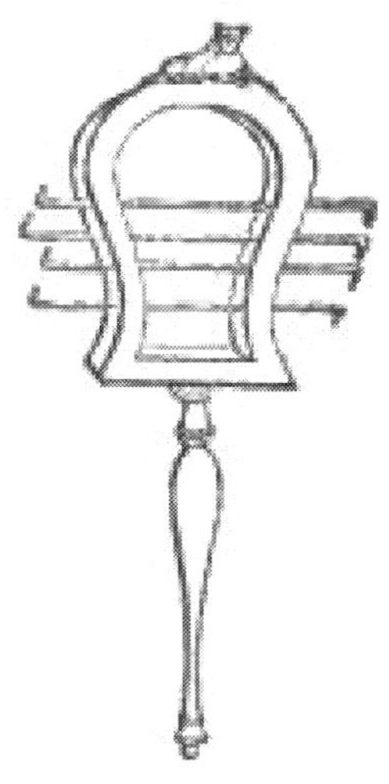

Trisyllables

u u u	Tribrach
- u u	Dactyl
u - u	Amphibrach
u u -	Anapest-Antidactylus
u - -	Bacchius
- - u	Antibacchius
- u -	Cretic-Amphimacer
- - -	Molossus

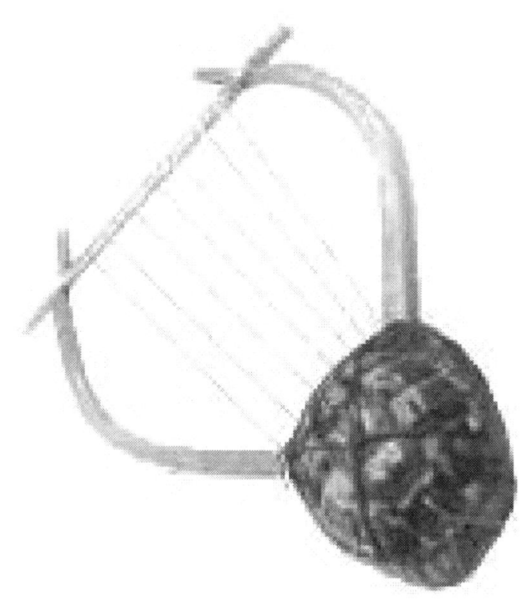

Tetrasyllables

u u u u	Tetrabrach-Proceleusmatic
- u u u	Primus paeon
u - u u	Secundus paeon
u u - u	Tertius paeon
u u u -	Quartus paeon
- - u u	Major ionic-Double trochee
u u - -	Minor ionic-Double iamb
- u - u	Ditrochee
u - u -	Diamb
- u u -	Choriamb
u - - u	Antispast
u - - -	First epitrite
- u - -	Second epitrite
- - u -	Third epitrite
- - - u	Fourth epitrite
- - - -	Dispondee

Pentasyllables

– – – – – – – – – –

u u u u u

– u u u u

– – u u u

– – – u u

– – – – u

– – – – –

u – – – –

u u – – –

u u u – –

u u u u –

Symbols

!+!

!0!

!1!

!2!

!3!

!4!

!5!

!D.C.!

!D.S.!

!accent!

!beambr1!

!beambr2!

!breath!

!coda!

!crescendo(!

!crescendo)!

!diminuendo(!

!diminuendo)!

!<(!

!<)!

!>(!

!>)!

!downbow!

!emphasis!

!>!

!fermata!

!f!

!ff!

!fff!

!ffff!

!fine!

!invertedfermata!

!longphrase!

!lowermordent!

!mediumphrase!

!mf!

!mordent!

!mp!

!open!

!p!

!pp!

!ppp!

!pppp!

!plus!

!pralltriller!

!roll!

!segno!

!sfz!

!shortphrase!

!snap!

!tenuto!

!thumb!

!trem1!

!trem2!

!trem3!

!trem4!

!trill!

!turn!

!upbow!

!uppermordent!

!wedge!

!turnx!

!invertedturn!

!invertedturnx!

!arpeggio!

!trill(!

!trill)!

Symbols

!+! !0! !1! !2! !3! !4! !5! !D.C.! !D.S.!
!accent! !beambr1! !beambr2! !breath!
!coda!
0 1 2 3 4 5 D.C. D.S. ,
!crescendo(! !crescendo)! !diminuendo(!
!diminuendo)! !<(! !<)! !>(! !>)!
!downbow! !emphasis! !>! !fermata! !f!
!ff! !fff! !ffff! !fine!
f ff fff ffff FINE
!invertedfermata! !longphrase!
!lowermordent! !mediumphrase! !mf!
!mordent! !mp! !open! !p!
mf mp p
!pp! !ppp! !pppp! !plus! !pralltriller!
!roll! !segno! !sfz! !shortphrase!
pp ppp pppp sfz
!snap! !tenuto! !thumb! !trem1! !trem2!
!trem3! !trem4! !trill!
tr
!turn! !upbow! !uppermordent! !wedge!
!turnx! !invertedturn! !invertedturnx!
!arpeggio! !trill(! !trill)!

```
67 symbols
-------
998 data
!+!,!0!,!1!,!2!,!3!,!4!,!5!,!D.C.!,!D.S.!
,!accent!,!beambr1!,!beambr2!,!breath!,!co
da!
,!crescendo(!,!crescendo)!,!diminuendo(!,!
diminuendo)!,!<(!,!<)!,!>(!,!>)!,!downbow!
,!emphasis!,!>!,!fermata!,!f!,!ff!,!fff!,!ffff
!,!fine!,!invertedfermata!,!longphrase!,!lo
wermordent!,!mediumphrase!,!mf!,!mord
ent!,!mp!,!open!
999 data
!p!,!pp!,!ppp!,!pppp!,!plus!,!pralltriller!,!
roll!,!segno!,!sfz!,!shortphrase!,!snap!,!te
nuto!,!thumb!,!trem1!,!trem2!,!trem3!,!tr
em4!,!trill!,!turn!,!upbow!,!uppermorden
t!,!wedge!,!turnx!,!invertedturn!,!inverte
dturnx!,!arpeggio!,!trill(!,!trill)!
```

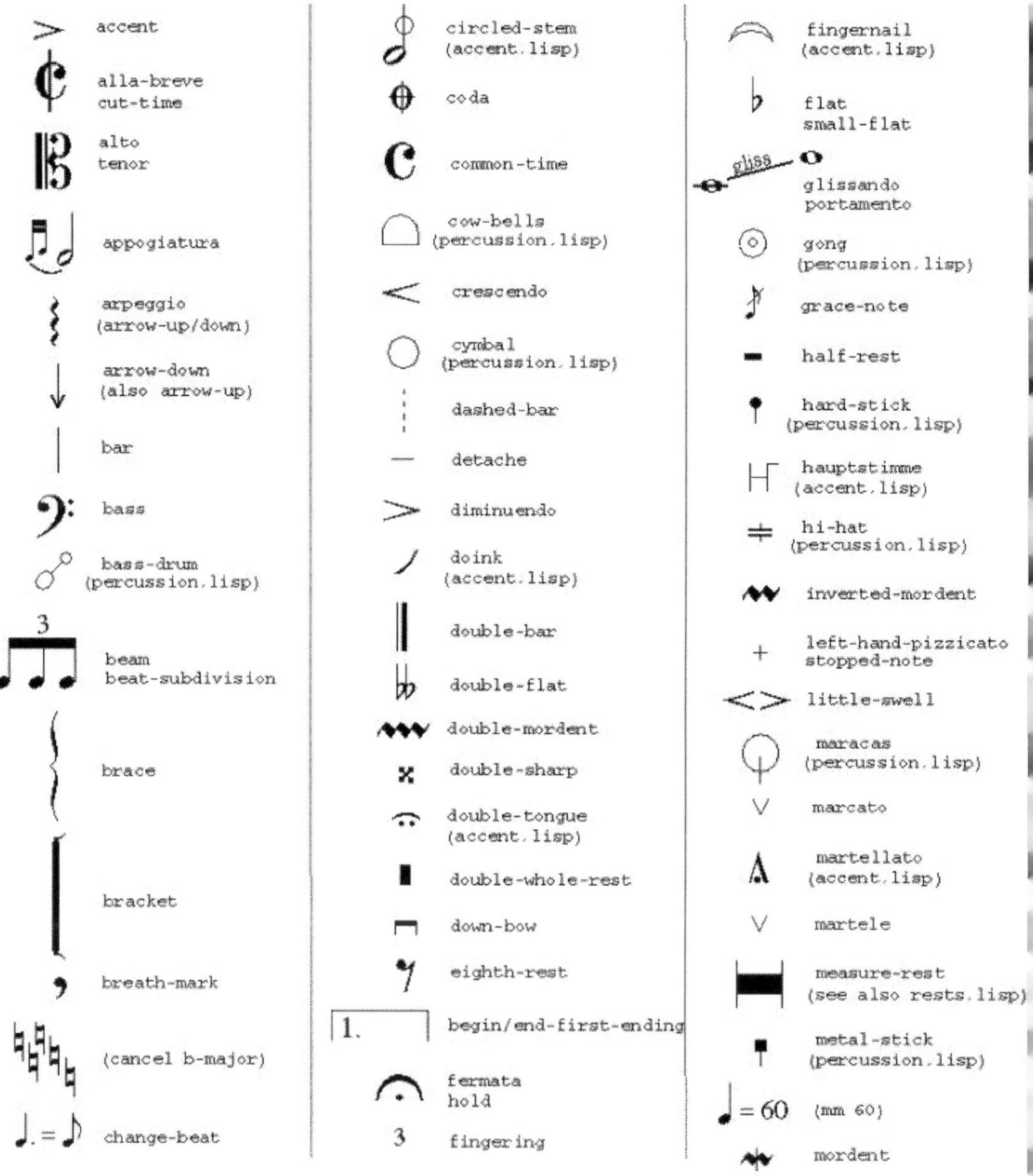

accent
alla-breve
cut-time
alto
tenor
appogiatura
arpeggio
(arrow-up/down)
arrow-down
(also arrow-up)
bar
bass
bass-drum
(percussion.lisp)
3
beam
beat-subdivision
brace
bracket
breath-mark
(cancel b-major)
change-beat
circled-stem
(accent.lisp)
coda
common-time
cow-bells
(percussion.lisp)
crescendo
cymbal
(percussion.lisp)
dashed-bar
detache
diminuendo
doink
(accent.lisp)
double-bar
double-flat
double-mordent
double-sharp
double-tongue
(accent.lisp)
double-whole-rest
down-bow
eighth-rest
1.
begin/end-first-ending
fermata
hold
3
fingering
fingernail
(accent.lisp)
flat
small-flat
gliss
glissando
portamento
gong
(percussion.lisp)
grace-note
half-rest
hard-stick
(percussion.lisp)
hauptstimme
(accent.lisp)
hi-hat
(percussion.lisp)
inverted-mordent
left-hand-pizzicato
stopped-note
little-swell
maracas
(percussion.lisp)
marcato
martellato
(accent.lisp)
martele
measure-rest
(see also rests.lisp)
metal-stick
(percussion.lisp)
= 60
(mm 60)
mordent

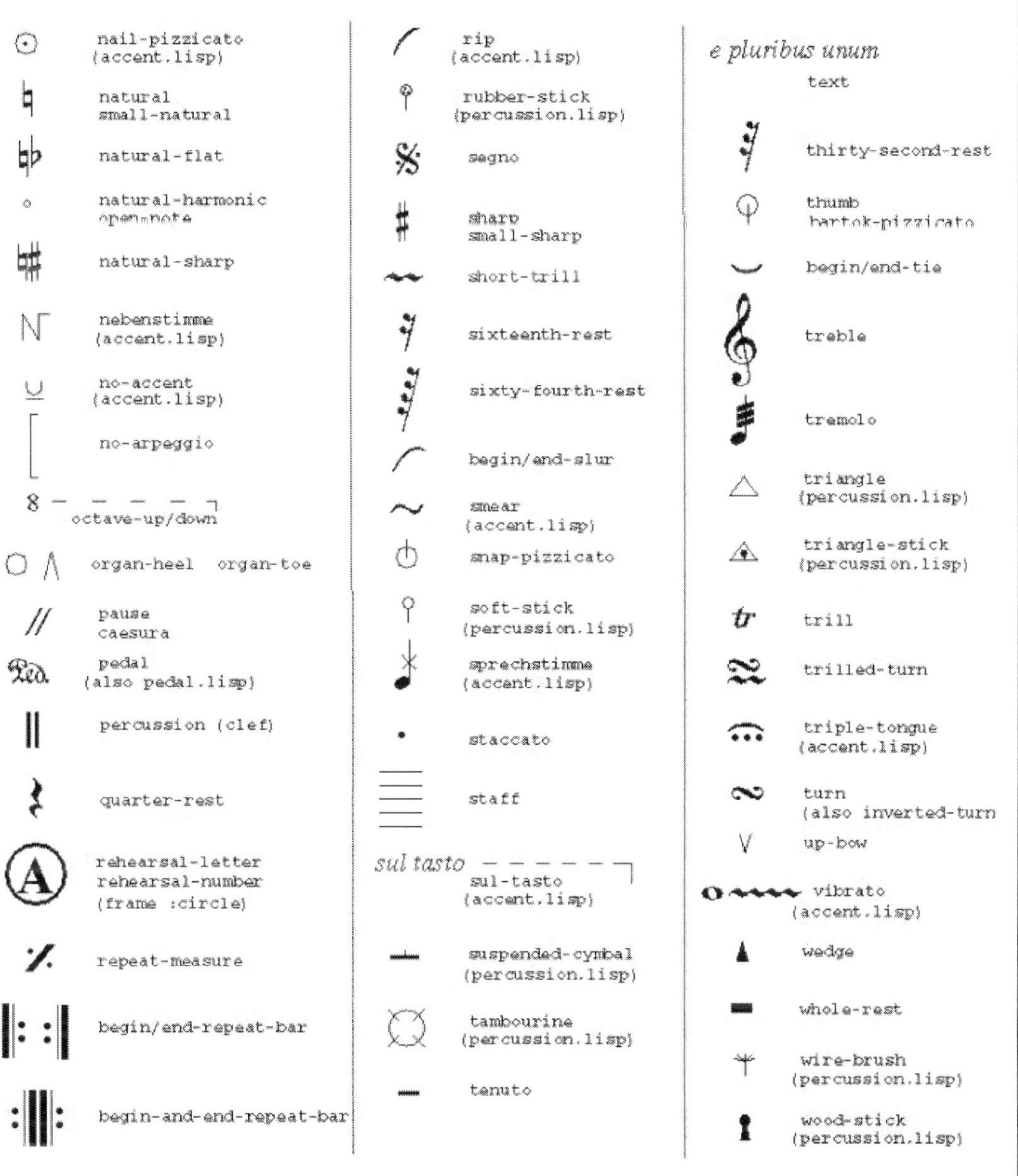
nail-pizzicato
(accent.lisp)
natural
small-natural
natural-flat
natural-harmonic
open-note
natural-sharp
nebenstimme
(accent.lisp)
no-accent
(accent.lisp)
no-arpeggio
8
octave-up/down
organ-heel organ-toe
pause
caesura
pedal
(also pedal.lisp)
percussion (clef)
quarter-rest
A
rehearsal-letter
rehearsal-number
(frame :circle)
repeat-measure
begin/end-repeat-bar
begin-and-end-repeat-bar
rip
(accent.lisp)
rubber-stick
(percussion.lisp)
segno
sharp
small-sharp
short-trill
sixteenth-rest
sixty-fourth-rest
begin/end-slur
smear
(accent.lisp)
snap-pizzicato
soft-stick
(percussion.lisp)
sprechstimme
(accent.lisp)
staccato
staff
sul tasto
sul-tasto
(accent.lisp)
suspended-cymbal
(percussion.lisp)
tambourine
(percussion.lisp)
tenuto
e pluribus unum
text
thirty-second-rest
thumb
bartok-pizzicato
begin/end-tie
treble
tremolo
triangle
(percussion.lisp)
triangle-stick
(percussion.lisp)
tr
trill
trilled-turn
triple-tongue
(accent.lisp)
turn
(also inverted-turn
up-bow
vibrato
(accent.lisp)
wedge
whole-rest
wire-brush
(percussion.lisp)
wood-stick
(percussion.lisp)

Major scale

C D E F G A B C
C# D# F F# G# A# C C#
D E F# G A B C# D
D# F G G# A# C D D#
E F# G# A B C# D# E
F G A A# C D E F
F# G# A# B C# D# F F#
G A B C D E F# G
G# A# C C# D# F G G#
A B C# D E F# G# A
A# C D D# F G A A#
B C# D# E F# G# A# B

Doric Mode

C D D# F G A A# C
C# D# E F# G# A# B C#
D E F G A B C D
D# F F# G# A# C C# D#
E F# G A B C# D E
F G G# A# C D D# F
F# G# A B C# D# E F#
G A A# C D E F G
G# A# B C# D# F F# G#
A B C D E F# G A
A# C C# D# F G G# A#
B C# D E F# G# A B

Phrygian Mode

C C# D# F G G# A# C
C# D E F# G# A B C#
D D# F G A A# C D
D# E F# G# A# B C# D#
E F G A B C D E
F F# G# A# C C# D# F
F# G A B C# D E F#
G G# A# C D D# F G
G# A B C# D# E F# G#
A A# C D E F G A
A# B C# D# F F# G# A#
B C D E F# G A B

Lydian Mode

C D E F# G A B C
C# D# F G G# A# C C#
D E F# G# A B C# D
D# F G A A# C D D#
E F# G# A# B C# D# E
F G A B C D E F
F# G# A# C C# D# F F#
G A B C# D E F# G
G# A# C D D# F G G#
A B C# D# E F# G# A
A# C D E F G A A#
B C# D# F F# G# A# B

Mysolidian Mode

C D E F G A A# C
C# D# F F# G# A# B C#
D E F# G A B C D
D# F G G# A# C C# D#
E F# G# A B C# D E
F G A A# C D D# F
F# G# A# B C# D# E F#
G A B C D E F G
G# A# C C# D# F F# G#
A B C# D E F# G A
A# C D D# F G G# A#
B C# D# E F# G# A B

Eolian Mode

C D D# F G G# A# C
C# D# E F# G# A B C#
D E F G A A# C D
D# F F# G# A# B C# D#
E F# G A B C D E
F G G# A# C C# D# F
F# G# A B C# D E F#
G A A# C D D# F G
G# A# B C# D# E F# G#
A B C D E F G A
A# C C# D# F F# G# A#
B C# D E F# G A B

Locrian Mode

C C# D# F F# G# A# C
C# D E F# G A B C#
D D# F G G# A# C D
D# E F# G# A B C# D#
E F G A A# C D E
F F# G# A# B C# D# F
F# G A B C D E F#
G G# A# C C# D# F G
G# A B C# D E F# G#
A A# C D D# F G A
A# B C# D# E F# G# A#
B C D E F G A B

Natural Minor Scale

C D D# F G G# A# C
C# D# E F# G# A B C#
D E F G A A# C D
D# F F# G# A# B C# D#
E F# G A B C D E
F G G# A# C C# D# F
F# G# A B C# D E F#
G A A# C D D# F G
G# A# B C# D# E F# G#
A B C D E F G A
A# C C# D# F F# G# A#
B C# D E F# G A B

Harmonic Minor Scale

C D D# F G G# B C
C# D# E F# G# A C C#
D E F G A A# C# D
D# F F# G# A# B D D#
E F# G A B C D# E
F G G# A# C C# E F
F# G# A B C# D F F#
G A A# C D D# F# G
G# A# B C# D# E G G#
A B C D E F G# A
A# C C# D# F F# A A#
B C# D E F# G A# B

Locrian 6 "Bequadro" (no altered)

C C# D# F F# A A# C
C# D E F# G A# B C#
D D# F G G# B C D
D# E F# G# A C C# D#
E F G A A# C# D E
F F# G# A# B D D# F
F# G A B C D# E F#
G G# A# C C# E F G
G# A B C# D F F# G#
A A# C D D# F# G A
A# B C# D# E G G# A#
B C D E F G# A B

Major 5#

C D E F G# A B C
C# D# F F# A A# C C#
D E F# G A# B C# D
D# F G G# B C D D#
E F# G# A C C# D# E
F G A A# C# D E F
F# G# A# B D D# F F#
G A B C D# E F# G
G# A# C C# E F G G#
A B C# D F F# G# A
A# C D D# F# G A A#
B C# D# E G G# A# B

Lidian Diminished

C D D# F# G A A# C
C# D# E G G# A# B C#
D E F G# A B C D
D# F F# A A# C C# D#
E F# G A# B C# D E
F G G# B C D D# F
F# G# A C C# D# E F#
G A A# C# D E F G
G# A# B D D# F F# G#
A B C D# E F# G A
A# C C# E F G G# A#
B C# D F F# G# A B

Spanish Scale

C C# E F G G# A# C
C# D F F# G# A B C#
D D# F# G A A# C D
D# E G G# A# B C# D#
E F G# A B C D E
F F# A A# C C# D# F
F# G A# B C# D E F#
G G# B C D D# F G
G# A C C# D# E F# G#
A A# C# D E F G A
A# B D D# F F# G# A#
B C D# E F# G A B

Lydian 2#

C D# E F# G A B C
C# E F G G# A# C C#
D F F# G# A B C# D
D# F# G A A# C D D#
E G G# A# B C# D# E
F G# A B C D E F
F# A A# C C# D# F F#
G A# B C# D E F# G
G# B C D D# F G G#
A C C# D# E F# G# A
A# C# D E F G A A#
B D D# F F# G# A# B

SuperLocrian bb7

C C# D# E F# G# A C
C# D E F G A A# C#
D D# F F# G# A# B D
D# E F# G A B C D#
E F G G# A# C C# E
F F# G# A B C# D F
F# G A A# C D D# F#
G G# A# B C# D# E G
G# A B C D E F G#
A A# C C# D# F F# A
A# B C# D E F# G A#
B C D D# F G G# B

Melodic Minor Scale

C D D# F G A B C
C# D# E F# G# A# C C#
D E F G A B C# D
D# F F# G# A# C D D#
E F# G A B C# D# E
F G G# A# C D E F
F# G# A B C# D# F F#
G A A# C D E F# G
G# A# B C# D# F G G#
A B C D E F# G# A
A# C C# D# F G A A#
B C# D E F# G# A# B

Doric 2b

C C# D# F G A A# C C
C# D E F# G# A# B C# C#
D D# F G A B C D D
D# E F# G# A# C C# D# D#
E F G A B C# D E E
F F# G# A# C D D# F F
F# G A B C# D# E F# F#
G G# A# C D E F G G
G# A B C# D# F F# G# G#
A A# C D E F# G A A
A# B C# D# F G G# A# A#
B C D E F# G# A B B

Lydian Augmented

C D E F# G# A B C
C# D# F G A A# C C#
D E F# G# A# B C# D
D# F G A B C D D#
E F# G# A# C C# D# E
F G A B C# D E F
F# G# A# C D D# F F#
G A B C# D# E F# G
G# A# C D E F G G#
A B C# D# F F# G# A
A# C D E F# G A A#
B C# D# F G G# A# B

Lydian Dominant

C D E F# G A A# C
C# D# F G G# A# B C#
D E F# G# A B C D
D# F G A A# C C# D#
E F# G# A# B C# D E
F G A B C D D# F
F# G# A# C C# D# E F#
G A B C# D E F G
G# A# C D D# F F# G#
A B C# D# E F# G A
A# C D E F G G# A#
B C# D# F F# G# A B

Myxolidian 6b

C D E F G G# A# C
C# D# F F# G# A B C#
D E F# G A A# C D
D# F G G# A# B C# D#
E F# G# A B C D E
F G A A# C C# D# F
F# G# A# B C# D E F#
G A B C D D# F G
G# A# C C# D# E F# G#
A B C# D E F G A
A# C D D# F F# G# A#
B C# D# E F# G A B

Locrian 2#

C D D# F F# G# A# C
C# D# E F# G A B C#
D E F G G# A# C D
D# F F# G# A B C# D#
E F# G A A# C D E
F G G# A# B C# D# F
F# G# A B C D E F#
G A A# C C# D# F G
G# A# B C# D E F# G#
A B C D D# F G A
A# C C# D# E F# G# A#
B C# D E F G A B

Superlocrian

C C# D# E F# G# A# C
C# D E F G A B C#
D D# F F# G# A# C D
D# E F# G A B C# D#
E F G G# A# C D E
F F# G# A B C# D# F
F# G A A# C D E F#
G G# A# B C# D# F G
G# A B C D E F# G#
A A# C C# D# F G A
A# B C# D E F# G# A#
B C D D# F G A B

Diminished W/H Tone

C D D# F F# G# A B C
C# D# E F# G A A# C C#
D E F G G# A# B C# D
D# F F# G# A B C D D#
E F# G A A# C C# D# E
F G G# A# B C# D E F
F# G# A B C D D# F F#
G A A# C C# D# E F# G
G# A# B C# D E F G G#
A B C D D# F F# G# A
A# C C# D# E F# G A A#
B C# D E F G G# A# B

Diminished H/W Tone

C C# D# E F# G A A# C
C# D E F G G# A# B C#
D D# F F# G# A B C D
D# E F# G A A# C C# D#
E F G G# A# B C# D E
F F# G# A B C D D# F
F# G A A# C C# D# E F#
G G# A# B C# D E F G
G# A B C D D# F F# G#
A A# C C# D# E F# G A
A# B C# D E F G G# A#
B C D D# F F# G# A B

Major Pentatonic

C D E G A C
C# D# F G# A# C#
D E F# A B D
D# F G A# C D#
E F# G# B C# E
F G A C D F
F# G# A# C# D# F#
G A B D E G
G# A# C D# F G#
A B C# E F# A
A# C D F G A#
B C# D# F# G# B

Minor Pentatonic

C D# F G A# C
C# E F# G# B C#
D F G A C D
D# F# G# A# C# D#
E G A B D E
F G# A# C D# F
F# A B C# E F#
G A# C D F G
G# B C# D# F# G#
A C D E G A
A# C# D# F G# A#
B D E F# A B

Blues Major Scale

C D D# E G A C
C# D# E F G# A# C#
D E F F# A B D
D# F F# G A# C D#
E F# G G# B C# E
F G G# A C D F
F# G# A A# C# D# F#
G A A# B D E G
G# A# B C D# F G#
A B C C# E F# A
A# C C# D F G A#
B C# D D# F# G# B

Blues Minor Scale

C D# F F# G A# C
C# E F# G G# B C#
D F G G# A C D
D# F# G# A A# C# D#
E G A A# B D E
F G# A# B C D# F
F# A B C C# E F#
G A# C C# D F G
G# B C# D D# F# G#
A C D D# E G A
A# C# D# E F G# A#
B D E F F# A B

Blues Altered Scale

C D D# E F F# G A A# C
C# D# E F F# G G# A# B C#
D E F F# G G# A B C D
D# F F# G G# A A# C C# D#
E F# G G# A A# B C# D E
F G G# A A# B C D D# F
F# G# A A# B C C# D# E F#
G A A# B C C# D E F G
G# A# B C C# D D# F F# G#
A B C C# D D# E F# G A
A# C C# D D# E F G G# A#
B C# D D# E F F# G# A B

60 REM ancient Greek modes
66 REM 1 aeo Greek Aeolian note : C-D-Eb-F-G-Ab-Bb-C * A Aeolian mode A [La] B [Ti] C [Do] D [Re] E [Mi] F [Fa] G [Sol] A [La] B [Ti]
70 REM 2 ion Greek Ionian note : C-D-E-F-G-A-B-C-D * C Ionian mode C, D, E, F, G, A, B, C (Do, Re, Mi, Fa, Sol, La, Ti, Do)
80 REM 3 lyd Greek Lydian note : c d e f g a b c d * F Lydian mode F, G, A, B, C, D, E, F (Fa, Sol, La, Ti, Do, Re, Mi, Fa)
90 REM 4 dor Greek Dorian note : e f g a b c d e f * D Dorian mode D, E, F, G, A, B, C, D (Re, Mi, Fa, Sol, La, Ti, Do, Re)
100 REM 5 mixo Greek Mixolydian note : b c d e f g a b c
110 REM 6 phry Greek Phrygian note : d e f g a b c d e * E Phrygian mode F, G, A, B, C, D, E (Mi, Fa, Sol, La, Ti, Do, Re, Mi)
120 REM 7 loc Greek B Locrian note : b c d e f g a b c * B Locrian mode Ti [B] Do [C] Re [D] Mi [E] Fa [F] Sol [G] La [A] Ti [B] C [Do]
140 REM 8 hdor Greek Hypodorian note : a b c d e f g a b * A [La] B [Ti] C [Do] D [Re] E [Mi] F [Fa] G [Sol] A [La] B [Ti]
150 REM 9 hlyd Greek Hypolydian note : f g a b c d e f g * F [Fa] G [Sol] A [La] B [Ti] C [Do] D [Re] E [Mi] F [Fa] G [Sol]

160 REM 10 hphr Greek Hypophrygian note : g a b c d e f g a * G [Sol] A [La] B [Ti] C [Do] D [Re] E [Mi] F [Fa] G [Sol] A [La]
170 REM 11 ydor Greek Yperdorian note : b c d e f g a b c (+ 4 notes from the normal)
180 REM 12 yloc Greek B Locrian note : F G A B C D E f g (+ 4 notes from the normal)
190 REM 13 ymixo Greek Mixolydian note : f g a b c d e f g (+ 4 notes from the normal)
200 REM 14 yphry Greek Phrygian note : a b c d e f g a b (+ 4 notes from the normal)
210 REM 15 yaeo Greek Aeolian note : G-Ab-Bb-C-D-Eb-F (+ 4 notes from the normal)
220 REM 16 yion Greek Ionian note : G-A-B-C-D-E-F-g-a (+ 4 notes from the normal)
230 REM 17 ylyd Greek Lydian note : g a b c d e f-g-a (+ 4 notes from the normal)

Major

Cb	Cb Db Eb Fb Gb Ab Bb Cb
Gb	Gb Ab Bb C Db Eb F Gb
Db	Db Eb F Gb Ab Bb C Db
Ab	Ab Bb C Db Eb F G Ab
Eb	Es F G Ab Bb C D Eb
Bb	Bb C D Eb F G A Bb
F	F G A Bb C D E F
C	C D E F G A B C
G	G A B C D E F# G
D	D E F# G A B C# D
A	A B C# D E F# G# A
E	E F# G# A B C# D# E
B	B C# D# E F# G# A# B
F#	F# G# A# B C# D# E# F#
C#	C# D# E# F# G# A# B# C#

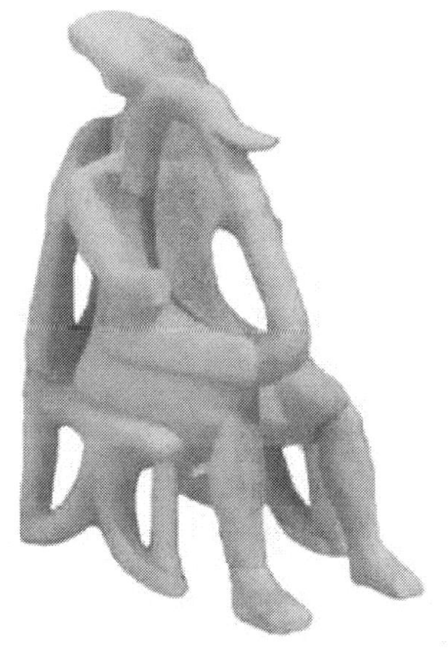

Melodic Minor

Cb	Ab Bb Cb Db Eb F G Ab
Gb	Eb F Gb Ab Bb C D Eb
Db	Bb C Db Eb F G A Bb
Ab	F G Ab Bb C D E F
Eb	C D Eb F G A B C
Bb	G A Bb C D E F# G
F	D E F G A B C# D
C	A B C D E F# G# A
G	E F# G A B C# D# E
D	B C# D E F# G# A# B
A	F# G# A B C# D# E# F#
E	C# D# E F# G# A# B# C#
B	G# A# B C# D# E# Fx G#
F#	D# E# F# G# A# B# Cx D#
C#	A# B# C# D# E# Fx Gx A#

Harmonic Minor

Cb	Ab Bb Cb Db Eb Fb G Ab
Gb	Eb F Gb Ab Bb Cb D Eb
Db	Bb C Db Eb F Gb A Bb
Ab	F G Ab Bb C Db E F
Eb	C D Eb F G Ab B C
Bb	G A Bb C D Eb F# G
F	D E F G A Bb C# D
C	A B C D E F G# A
G	E F# G A B C D# E
D	B C# D E F# G A# B
A	F# G# A B C# D E# F#
E	C# D# E F# G# A B# C#
B	G# A# B C# D# E Fx G#
F#	D# E# F# G# A# B Cx D#
C#	A# B# C# D# F# Gx A#

Natural Minor

Cb	Ab Bb Cb Db Eb Fb Gb Ab
Gb	Eb F Gb Ab Bb Cb Db Eb
Db	Bb C Db Eb F Gb Ab Bb
Ab	F G Ab Bb C Db Eb F
Eb	C D Eb F G Ab Bb C
Bb	G A Bb C D Eb F G
F	D E F G A Bb C D
C	A B C D E F G A
G	E F# G A B C D E
D	B C# D E F# G A B
A	F# G# A B C# D E F#
E	C# D# E F# G# A B C#
B	G # A# B C# D# E F# G#
F#	D# E# F# G# A# B C# D#
C#	A# B# C# D# E# F# G# A#

18 new notes

Hamsadhwani,E,^F,^G,B,^D,E,^F,^G,B
Revathi,E,F,A,B,D,E,F,A,B
Abhogi,E,^F,G,A,^C,E,^F,G,A
Vasantha,E,^GA,^C,^D,F,E,^GA,^C,^D
Mayamalavagoula,E,F,^GA,B,C,^D,E,F,^GA
Niroshta,E,^F,^G,^C,^D,E,^F,^G,^C
Amrithavarshini,E,^G,^A,B,^D,E,^G,^A,B
Nata like,E,G,^G,A,B,^D,E,G,^G
Gambheera Nata,E,^G,A,B,^D,E,^G,A,B
Charukesi,E,^F,^G,A,B,C,D,E,^F
Hemavathi,E,^F,G,^A,B,^C,D,E,^F
Lathangi,E,^F,^G,^A,B,C,^D,E,^F
Kanakangi,E,F,^F,A,B,C,^C,E,F
Like Varali,E,F,^F,^A,B,C,^D,E,F
Chakravaham,E,F,^G,A,B,^C,D,E,F
Bhoopala or morning
raga,E,F,^G,B,C,E,F,^G,B
Purvi kalyani like,E,F,^G,^A,B,^C,^D,F,^G
Like what?,E,F,^G,A,B,^C,^D,E,F

Εἰσὶ δὲ οἱ μὲν ἐν τῷ διατόνῳ <φθόγγοι> οἵδε

1. προσλαμβανόμενος
2. ὑπάτη ὑπάτων
3. παρυπάτη ὑπάτων
4. λιχανὸς ὑπάτων διάτονος
5. ὑπάτη μέσων
6. παρυπάτη μέσων
7. λιχανὸς μέσων διάτονος
8. μέση
9. τρίτη συνημμένων
10. παρανήτη συνημμένων διάτονος
11. νήτη συνημμένων
12. παραμέση
13. τρίτη διεζευγμένων
14. παρανήτη διεζευγμένων διάτονος
15. νήτη διεζευγμένων
16. τρίτη ὑπερβολαίων
17. παρανήτη ὑπερβολαίων διάτονος
18. νήτη ὑπερβολαίων.

Ἐν δὲ χρώματι οἵδε

1. προσλαμβανόμενος
2. ὑπάτη ὑπάτων
3. παρυπάτη ὑπάτων
4. λιχανὸς ὑπάτων χρωματική
5. ὑπάτη μέσων
6. παρυπάτη μέσων
7. λιχανὸς μέσων χρωματική
8. μέση
9. τρίτη συνημμένων
10. παρανήτη συνημμένων χρωματική
11. νήτη συνημμένων
12. παραμέση
13. τρίτη διεζευγμένων
14. παρανήτη διεζευγμένων χρωματική
15. νήτη διεζευγμένων
16. τρίτη ὑπερβολαίων
17. παρανήτη ὑπερβολαίων χρωματική
18. νήτη ὑπερβολαίων.

Ἐν δὲ ἁρμονίᾳ οἵδε

1. προσλαμβανόμενος
2. ὑπάτη ὑπάτων
3. παρυπάτη ὑπάτων
4. λιχανὸς ὑπάτων ἐναρμόνιος
5. ὑπάτη μέσων
6. παρυπάτη μέσων
7. λιχανὸς μέσων ἐναρμόνιος
8. μέση
9. τρίτη συνημμένων ἐναρμόνιος
10. παρανήτη συνημμένων ἐναρμόνιος
11. νήτη συνημμένων
12. παραμέση
13. τρίτη διεζευγμένων ἐναρμόνιος
14. παρανήτη διεζευγμένων ἐναρμόνιος
15. νήτη διεζευγμένων
16. τρίτη ὑπερβολαίων ἐναρμόνιος
17. παρανήτη ὑπερβολαίων ἐναρμόνιος
18. νήτη ὑπερβολαίων.

Κατὰ δὲ μίξιν τῶν γενῶν οἵδε

1. προσλαμβανόμενος
2. ὑπάτη ὑπάτων
3. παρυπάτη ὑπάτων
4. λιχανὸς ὑπάτων ἐναρμόνιος
5. λιχανὸς ὑπάτων χρωματική
6. λιχανὸς ὑπάτων διάτονος
7. ὑπάτη μέσων
8. παρυπάτη μέσων
9. λιχανὸς μέσων ἐναρμόνιος
10. λιχανὸς μέσων χρωματική
11. λιχανὸς μέσων διάτονος
12. μέση
13. τρίτη συνημμένων
14. παρανήτη συνημμένων ἐναρμόνιος
15. παρανήτη συνημμένων χρωματική
16. παρανήτη συνημμένων διάτονος
17. νήτη συνημμένων
18. παραμέση
19. τρίτη διεζευγμένων
20. παρανήτη διεζευγμένων ἐναρμόνιος
21. παρανήτη διεζευγμένων χρωματική
22. παρανήτη διεζευγμένων διάτονος
23. νήτη διεζευγμένων
24. τρίτη ὑπερβολαίων
25. παρανήτη ὑπερβολαίων ἐναρμόνιος
26. παρανήτη ὑπερβολαίων χρωματική
27. παρανήτη ὑπερβολαίων διάτονος
28. νήτη ὑπερβολαίων.

Lyric Genres

Hymn
Hyporcheme
Prosodion
Paean
Dithyramb
Enkomion
Epinikion
Skolion
Erotikon
Hymenaios
Threnos
Partheneion

Arabian,A,B,C,D,_E,F,^F,^G,A
Hindustan,A,B,^C,D,E,F,G,A,B
Persian,A,_B,^C,D,E,F,^G,A,_B,^C
Romanian,A,B,C,^D,E,^F,G,A,B,C
Hungarian Major,A,C,^C,^D,E,^F,G,A,C
Scriabin,A,_B,^C,E,^F,A,_B,^C,E,^F
Egyptian,A,B,D,E,G,A,B,D,E
Japanese,A,_B,D,E,F,A,_B,D,E
Chinese,A,^C,^D,E,^G,A,^C,^D,E
Iwato Japan,A,_B,D,_E,G,A,_B,D,_E
Kokin Joshi Japan,A,_B,D,E,G,A,_B,D,E
P'Yongio,A,B,D,E,^F,G,A,B,D
Pelog,A,_B,C,E,F,A,_B,C,E
Oriental,A,_B,^C,D,_E,^F,G,A,_B
Arabian,C,D,_E,F,_G,^G,A,B,C
Gypsy,A,B,C,^D,E,F,^G,A,B
Romanian,D,E,F,^G,A,B,C,D,E
Indian,E,F,B,G,C,E,F,B,G
Persian,E,F,^G,A,_B,C,^D,E,F
Byzantine,E,F,^G,A,B,C,^D,E,F
Oriental,G,A,_B,C,_D,E,F,G,A
Jewish,E,F,^G,A,B,C,D,E,F
Japanese,G,A,B,D,_E,G,A,B,D

Shostakovich name in Cyrillic monogram
(9-39-1)
Key C

C C# D# E F# G A B
Triads in Scale: C A B D#m Em F#m Am G C#dim
D#dim F#dim

Key G

G G# A# B C# D E F#
Triads in Scale: G E F# A#m Bm C#m Em D G#dim
A#dim C#dim

Key D

D D# E# F# G# A B C#
Triads in Scale: D B C# E#m F#m G#m Bm A
D#dim E#dim G#dim

Key A

A A# B# C# D# E F# G#
Triads in Scale: A F# G# B#m C#m D#m F#m E
A#dim B#dim D#dim

Key E

E E# F## G# A# B C# D#
Triads in Scale: E C# D# F##m G#m A#m C#m B
E#dim F##dim A#dim

Key B

B B# C## D# E# F# G# A#
Triads in Scale: B G# A# C##m D#m E#m G#m F# B#dim C##dim E#dim

Key F#

F# F## G## A# B# C# D# E#
Triads in Scale: F# D# E# G##m A#m B#m D#m C# F##dim G##dim B#dim

Key F

F F# G# A B C D E
Triads in Scale: F D E G#m Am Bm Dm C F#dim G#dim Bdim

Key Bb

Bb B C# D E F G A
Triads in Scale: Bb G A C#m Dm Em Gm F Bdim C#dim Edim

Key Eb

Eb E F# G A Bb C D
Triads in Scale: Eb C D F#m Gm Am Cm Bb Edim F#dim Adim

Key Ab

Ab A B C D Eb F G
Triads in Scale: Ab F G Bm Cm Dm Fm Eb Adim Bdim Ddim

Key Db

Db D E F G Ab Bb C
Triads in Scale: Db Bb C Em Fm Gm Bbm Ab Ddim Edim Gdim

Key Gb

Gb G A Bb C Db Eb F
Triads in Scale: Gb Eb F Am Bbm Cm Ebm Db Gdim Adim Cdim

105 x 12ˆ 1.260 different Musical Scales

----

12 Gods - Clefs

Treble K: treble
Treble 1̂8- K: treble-8
Treble 1̂8 K: treblë8
Bass K: bass
Baritone K: bass3
Tenor K: alto4
Alto K: alto
Mezzosoprano K: alto2
Soprano K: alto1
G on third line K: middlêG
no clef K: none
percussions K: perc

105 ancient Greek Key modes

----

7 Sharps Major Ionian C# C,D,E,F,G,A,B,C,D
6 Sharps Major Ionian F#
5 Sharps Major Ionian B
4 Sharps Major Ionian E
3 Sharps Major Ionian A
2 Sharps Major Ionian D
1 Sharps Major Ionian G
0 Sharps Major Ionian C
1 Flat Major Ionian F
2 Flat Major Ionian Bb
---
3 Flat Major Ionian Eb
4 Flat Major Ionian Ab
5 Flat Major Ionian Db
6 Flat Major Ionian Gb
7 Flat Major Ionian Cb
---
7 Sharps Minor Aeolian A#m C-D-Eb-F-G-Ab-Bb-Cb
6 Sharps Minor Aeolian D#m
5 Sharps Minor Aeolian G#m
4 Sharps Minor Aeolian C#m
3 Sharps Minor Aeolian F#m
2 Sharps Minor Aeolian Bm
1 Sharps Minor Aeolian Em
0 Sharps Minor Aeolian Am
1 Flat Minor Aeolian Dm
2 Flat Minor Aeolian Gm
3 Flat Minor Aeolian Cm
4 Flat Minor Aeolian Fm
5 Flat Minor Aeolian Bbm

6 Flat Minor Aeolian Ebm
7 Flat Minor Aeolian Abm
---
7 Sharps Mixolydian G#Mix B,C,D,E,F,G,A,B,C
6 Sharps Mixolydian C#Mix
5 Sharps Mixolydian F#Mix
4 Sharps Mixolydian BMix
3 Sharps Mixolydian EMix
2 Sharps Mixolydian AMix
1 Sharps Mixolydian DMix
0 Sharps Mixolydian GMix
1 Flat Mixolydian CMix
2 Flat Mixolydian FMix
3 Flat Mixolydian BbMix
4 Flat Mixolydian EbMix
5 Flat Mixolydian AbMix
6 Flat Mixolydian DbMix
7 Flat Mixolydian GbMix
---
7 Sharps Dorian D#Dor D, E, F, G, A, B, C, D
6 Sharps Dorian G#Dor
5 Sharps Dorian C#Dor
4 Sharps Dorian F#Dor
3 Sharps Dorian BDor
2 Sharps Dorian EDor
1 Sharps Dorian ADor
0 Sharps Dorian DDor
1 Flat Dorian GDor
2 Flat Dorian CDor
3 Flat Dorian FDor
4 Flat Dorian BbDor
5 Flat Dorian EbDor
6 Flat Dorian AbDor

7 Flat Dorian DbDor

---

7 Sharps Phrygian E#Phr F, G, A, B, C, D, E
6 Sharps Phrygian A#Phr
5 Sharps Phrygian D#Phr
4 Sharps Phrygian G#Phr
3 Sharps Phrygian C#Phr
2 Sharps Phrygian F#Phr
1 Sharps Phrygian BPhr
0 Sharps Phrygian EPhr
1 Flat Phrygian APhr
2 Flat Phrygian Dphr
3 Flat Phrygian GPhr
4 Flat Phrygian CPhr
5 Flat Phrygian FPhr
6 Flat Phrygian BbPhr
7 Flat Phrygian EbPhr

---

7 Sharps Lydian F#Lyd c,d,e,f,g,a,b,c,d
6 Sharps Lydian BLyd
5 Sharps Lydian ELyd
4 Sharps Lydian ALyd
3 Sharps Lydian DLyd
2 Sharps Lydian GLyd
1 Sharps Lydian CLyd
0 Sharps Lydian FLyd
1 Flat Lydian BbLyd
2 Flat Lydian EbLyd
3 Flat Lydian AbLyd
4 Flat Lydian DbLyd
5 Flat Lydian GbLyd
6 Flat Lydian CbLyd
7 Flat Lydian FbLyd

---

7 Sharps Locrian B#Loc b c d e f g a b c
6 Sharps Locrian E#Loc
5 Sharps Locrian A#Loc
4 Sharps Locrian D#Loc
3 Sharps Locrian G#Loc
2 Sharps Locrian C#Loc
1 Sharps Locrian F#Loc
0 Sharps Locrian BLoc
1 Flat Locrian ELoc
2 Flat Locrian ALoc
3 Flat Locrian DLoc
4 Flat Locrian GLoc
5 Flat Locrian CLoc
6 Flat Locrian FLoc
7 Flat Locrian BbLoc

105 ancient Greek modes x 12 clefŝ 1.260 different musics

C minor̂ C,D,Eb,F,G,Ab,Bb,C,D
D minor̂ D,E,F,G,A,Bb,C,D,E
E minor̂ E,^F,G,A,B,C,D,E,^F
F minor̂ F,G,Ab,Bb,C,Db,Eb,F,G
G minor̂ G,A,Bb,C,D,Eb,F,G,A
A minor̂ A,B,C,D,E,F,G,A,B
B minor̂ B,^C,D,E,^F,G,A,B,^C
C# minor̂ ^C,^D,E,^F,^G,A,B,^C,^D
Eb minor̂ Eb,F,Gb,Ab,Bb,Cb,Db,Eb,F
F# minor̂ ^F,^G,A,B,^C,D,E,^F,^G
G# minor̂ ^G,^A,B,^C,^D,E,^F,^G,^A
Bb minor̂ Bb,C,Db,Eb,F,Gb,Ab,Bb,C

Natural C Minor Scalê C,D,Eb,F,G,Ab,Bb,C,D
Harmonic C Minor Scalê C,D,Eb,F,G,Ab,B,C,D

Natural C Minor Scalê C,D,Eb,F,G,Ab,Bb,C,D
Melodic C Minor Scalê C,D,Eb,F,G,A,B,C,D

Technical name:

1 TONIC
2 SUPERTONIC
3 MEDIANT
4 SUBDOMINANT
5 DOMINANT
6 SUBMEDIANT
7 LEADING TONE

Major
_C,_D,_E,_F,_G,_A,_B,_C,_D
_G,_A,_B,C,_D,_E,F,_G,_A
_D,_E,F,_G,_A,_B,C,_D,
_A,_B,C,_D,_E,F,G,_A,
E,F,G,_A,_B,C,D,_E,
_B,C,D,_E,F,G,A,_B,
F,G,A,_B,C,D,E,F,
C,D,E,F,G,A,B,C,
G,A,B,C,D,E,^F,G,
D,E,^F,G,A,B,^C,D,
A,B,^C,D,E,^F,^G,A,
E,^F,^G,A,B,^C,^D,E,
B,^C,^D,E,^F,^G,^A,B,
^F,^G,^A,B,^C,^D,^E,^F,
^C,^D,^E,^F,^G,^A,^B,^C,

Melodic Minor
_A,_B,_C,_D,_E,F,G,_A,
_E,F,_G,_A,_B,C,D,_E,
_B,C,_D,_E,F,G,A,_B,
F,G,_A,_B,C,D,E,F,
C,D,_E,F,G,A,B,C,
G,A,_B,C, D,E,^F,G,
D,E,F,G,A,B,^C,D,
A,B,C,D,E,^F,^G,A,
E,^F,G,A,B,^C,^D,E,
B,^C,D,E,^F,^G,^A,B,
^F,^G,A,B,^C,^D,^E,^F,
^C,^D,E,^F,^G,^A,^B,^C,
^G,^A,B,^C,^D,^E,F,^G,
^D,^E,^F,^G,^A,^B,C,^D,
^A,^B,^C,^D,^E,F,G,^A,

Harmonic Minor
_A,_B,_C,_D,_E,_F,G,_A,
_E,F,_G,_A,_B,_C,D,_E,
_B,C,_D,_E,F,_G,A,_B,
F,G,_A,_B,C,_D,E,F,
C,D,_E,F,G,_A,B,C,
G,A,_B,C,D,_E,^F,G,
D,E,F,G,A,_B,^C,D,
A,B,C,D,E,F,^G,A,
E,^F,G,A,B,C,^D,E,
B,^C,D,E,^F,G,^A,B,
^F,^G,A,B,^C,D,^E,^F,
^C,^D,E,^F,^G,A,^B,^C,
^G,^A,B,^C,^D,E,F,^G,
^D,^E,^F,^G,^A,B,C,^D,
^A,^B,^C,^D,^F,G,^A,

Natural Minor
_A,_B,_C,_D,_E,_F,_G,_A,
_E,F,_G,_A,_B,_C,_D,_E,
_B,C,_D,_E,F,_G,_A,_B,
F,G,_A,_B,C,_D,_E,F,
C,D,_E,F,G,_A,_B,C,
G,A,_B,C,D,_E,F,G,
D,E,F,G,A,_B,C,D,
A,B,C,D,E,F,G,A,
E,^F,G,A,B,C,D,E,
B,^C,D,E,^F,G,A,B,
^F,^G,A,B,^C,D,E,^F,
^C,^D,E,^F,^G,A,B,^C,
^G,^A,B,^C,^D,E,^F,^G,
^D,^E,^F,^G,^A,B,^C,^D,
^A,^B,^C,^D,^E,^F,^G,^A,

4 modes

Ambrosian Modes
1st d e f g a b c d e
2nd e f g a b c d e f
3rd f g a b c d e f g
4th g a b c d e f g a

1st tone d,e,f,g,a,b,c,d
2nd tone e,f,g,a,b,c,d,e
3rd tone f,g,a,b,c,d,e,f
4th tone g,a,b,c,d,e,f,g

8 modes

Pope Gregory the Great added four more, which were known as 'plagal'.

Gregorian Modes
1st Authentic d e f g a b c d e
2nd Plagal a b c d e f g a b
3rd Authentic e f g a b c d e f
4th Plagal b c d e f g a b c
5th Authentic f g a b c d e f g
6th Plagal c d e f g a b c d
7th Authentic g a b c d e f g a
8th Plagal d e f g a b c d e

Gregorian Modes
1st tone Authentic D,e,f,g,a,b,c,d
2nd tone Plagal a,b,c,D,e,f,g,a
3rd tone Authentic E,f,g,a,b,c,d,e
4th tone Plagal b,c,d,E,f,g,a,b
5th tone Authentic F,g,a,b,c,d,e,f
6th tone Plagal c,d,e,F,g,a,b,c
7th tone Authentic G,a,b,c,d,e,f,g
8th tone Plagal d,e,f,G,a,b,c,d

7 modes

Renaissance Modes

Mode Name Notes Scale pattern

Ionian c,d,e,f,g,a,b 1 2 3 4 5 6 7

Dorian d,e,f,g,a,b,c 1 2 -3 4 5 6 -7

Phrygian e,f,g,a,b,c,d 1 -2 -3 4 5 -6 7

Lydian f,g,a,b,c,d,e 1 2 3 4 5 6 7

Mixolydian g,a,b,c,d,e,f 1 2 3 4 5 6 -7

Aeolian a,b,c,d,e,f,g 1 2 -3 4 5 -6 -7

Locrian b,c,d,e,f,g,a 1 -2 -3 4 -5 -6 -7

Renaissance Mode

Ionian c,d,e,f,g,a,b,c,d

Dorian d,e,f,g,a,b,c,d,e

Phrygian e,f,g,a,b,c,d,e,f

Lydian f,g,a,b,c,d,e,f,g

Mixolydian g,a,b,c,d,e,f,g,a

Aeolian a,b,c,d,e,f,g,a,b

Locrian b,c,d,e,f,g,a,b,c

7 modes

Renaissance Modes, C starting pitch
Mode Name Notes Scale pattern Key signature
Ionian C,D,E,F,G,A,B, 1 2 3 4 5 6 7 No flats or sharps
Dorian C,D,Eb,F,G,A,Bb 1 2 -3 4 5 6 -7 Bb Eb
Phrygian C,Db,Eb,F,G,Ab,Bb 1 -2 -3 4 5 -6 7 Bb Eb Ab Db
Lydian C,D,E,F#,G,A,B 1 2 3 4 5 6 7 F#
Mixolydian C,D,E,F,G,A,Bb 1 2 3 4 5 6 -7 Bb
Aeolian C,D,Eb,F,G,Ab,Bb 1 2 -3 4 5 -6 -7 Bb Eb Ab
Locrian C,Db,Eb,F,Gb,Ab,Bb 1 -2 -3 4 -5 -6 -7 Bb Eb Ab Db Gb

Renaissance Mode C
Ionian C,D,E,F,G,A,B,C,D
Dorian C,D,_E,F,G,A,_B,C,D
Phrygian C,_D,_E,F,G,_A,_B,C,_D
Lydian C,D,E,^F,G,A,B,C,D
Mixolydian C,D,E,F,G,A,_B,C,D
Aeolian C,D,_E,F,G,_A,_B,C,D
Locrian C,_D,_E,F,_G,_A,_B,C,_D

Accompaniment chords
----

minor m or min
major maj
diminished dim
augmented ¨ or aug
sustained sus
seventh,ninth,etc 7,9,...

Standard abbreviations
----

u !upbow!
v !downbow!
T !trill!
H !fermata!
L !accent! or !emphasis!
M !lowermordent!
P !uppermordent!
S !segno!
O !coda!

----
9 types
!upbow!,!downbow!,!trill!,!fermata!,!accent!,!lowermordent!,!uppermordent!,!segno!,!coda!

7 types
min,maj,dim,aug,sus,7,9

C Aeolian	C	D	Eb	F	G	Ab	Bb	C
F Aeolian	F	G	Ab	Bb	C	Db	Eb	F
Bb Aeolian	Bb	C	Db	Eb	F	Gb	Ab	Bb
Eb Aeolian	Eb	F	G	Ab	Bb	Cb	Db	Eb
G# Aeolian	G#	A#	B	C#	D#	E	F#	G#
C# Aeolian	C#	D#	E	F#	G#	A	B	Db
F# Aeolian	F#	G#	A	B	C#	D	E	F#
B Aeolian	B	C#	D	E	F#	G	A	B
E Aeolian	E	F#	G	A	B	C	D	E
A Aeolian	A	B	C	D	E	F	G	A
D Aeolian	D	E	F	G	A	Bb	C	D
G Aeolian	G	A	Bb	C	D	Eb	F	G

C minor^ C,D,Eb,F,G,Ab,Bb,C,D
D minor^ D,E,F,G,A,Bb,C,D,E
E minor^ E,^F,G,A,B,C,D,E,^F
F minor^ F,G,Ab,Bb,C,Db,Eb,F,G
G minor^ G,A,Bb,C,D,Eb,F,G,A
A minor^ A,B,C,D,E,F,G,A,B
B minor^ B,^C,D,E,^F,G,A,B,^C
C# minor^ ^C,^D,E,^F,^G,A,B,^C,^D
Eb minor^ Eb,F,Gb,Ab,Bb,Cb,Db,Eb,F
F# minor^ ^F,^G,A,B,^C,D,E,^F,^G
G# minor^ ^G,^A,B,^C,^D,E,^F,^G,^A
Bb minor^ Bb,C,Db,Eb,F,Gb,Ab,Bb,C

Ambrosian Modes	
1st tone	d e f g a b c d
2nd tone	e f g a b c d e
3rd tone	f g a b c d e f
4th tone	g a b c d e f g

Gregorian Modes		
1st tone	Authentic	De f g a b c d
2nd tone	Plagal	a b c D e f g a
3rd tone	Authentic	E f g a b c d e
4th tone	Plagal	b c d E f g a b
5th tone	Authentic	F g a b c d e f
6th tone	Plagal	c d e F g a b c
7th tone	Authentic	G a b c d e f g
8th tone	Plagal	d e f G a b c d

Renaissance Modes		
Mode Name	Notes	Scale pattern
Ionian	c d e f g a b	1 2 3 4 5 6 7
Dorian	d e f g a b c	1 2 -3 4 5 6 -7
Phrygian	e f g a b c d	1 -2 -3 4 5 -6 7
Lydian	f g a b c d e	1 2 3 +4 5 6 7
Mixolydian	g a b c d e f	1 2 3 4 5 6 -7
Aeolian	a b c d e f g	1 2 -3 4 5 -6 -7
Locrian	b c d e f g a	1 -2 -3 4 -5 -6 -7

Renaissance Modes, C starting pitch			
Mode Name	Notes	Scale pattern	Key signature
Ionian	C D E F G A B	1 2 3 4 5 6 7	No flats or sharps
Dorian	C D Eb F G A Bb	1 2 -3 4 5 6 -7	Bb Eb
Phrygian	C Db Eb F G Ab Bb	1 -2 -3 4 5 -6 7	Bb Eb Ab Db
Lydian	C D E F# G A B	1 2 3 +4 5 6 7	F#
Mixolydian	C D E F G A Bb	1 2 3 4 5 6 -7	Bb
Aeolian	C D Eb F G Ab Bb	1 2 -3 4 5 -6 -7	Bb Eb Ab
Locrian	C Db Eb F Gb Ab Bb	1 -2 -3 4 -5 -6 -7	Bb Eb Ab Db Gb

Blues Scale in all 12 Keys

A, C, D, D#, E, G, A
Bb, Db, Eb, E, F, Ab, Bb
B, D, E, E#, F#, A, B
C, Eb, F, F#, G, Bb, C
Db, Fb, Gb, G, Ab, Cb, Db
D, F, G, G#, A, C, D
Eb, Gb, Ab, A, Bb, Db, Eb
E, G, A, A#, B, D, E
F, Ab, Bb, B, C, Eb, F
F#, A, B, B#, C#, E, F#
G, Bb, C, C#, D, F, G
Ab, Cb, Db, D, Eb, Gb, Ab

Major Scales Method (2, 2, 1, 2, 2, 2, 1)

C Major- C, D, E, F, G, A, B, C
C# Major- C#, D#, F, F#, G#, A#, C, C#
Db Major- Db, Eb, F, Gb, Ab, Bb, C, Db
D Major- D, E, F#, G, A, B, C#, D
D# Major- D#, F, G, G#, A#, C, D, D#
Eb Major- Eb, F, G, Ab, Bb, C, D, Eb
E Major- E, F#, G#, A, B, C#, D#, E
F Major- F, G, A, Bb, C, D, E, F
F# Major- F#, G#, A#, B, C#, D#, E#, F#
Gb Major- Gb, Ab, Bb, Cb, Db, Eb, F, Gb
G Major- G, A, B, C, D, E, F#, G
Ab Major- Ab, Bb, C, Db, Eb, F, G, Ab
A Major- A, B, C#, D, E, F#, G#, A
Bb Major- Bb, C, D, Eb, F, G, A, Bb
B Major- B, C#, D#, E, F#, G#, A#, B
Cb Major- Cb, Db, Eb, Fb, Gb, Ab, Bb, Cb

Minor Scales (Natural) Method (2, 1, 2, 2, 1, 2, 2)

C Minor- C, D, Eb, F, G, Ab, Bb, C
C# Minor- C#, D#, E, F#, G#, A, B, C#
D Minor- D, E, F, G, A, Bb, C, D
D# Minor- D#, E#, F#, G#, A#, B, C#, D#
Eb Minor- Eb, F, Gb, Ab, Bb, Cb, Db, Eb
E Minor- E, F#, G, A, B, C, D, E
F Minor- F, G, Ab, Bb, C, Db, Eb, F
F# Minor- F#, G#, A, B, C#, D, E, F#
G Minor- G, A, Bb, C, D, Eb, F, G
G# Minor- G#, A#, B, C#, D#, E, F#, G#
Ab Minor- Ab, Bb, Cb, Db, Eb, Fb, Gb, Ab
A Minor- A, B, C, D, E, F, G, A
A# Minor- A#, B#, C#, D#, E#, F#, G#, A#
Bb Minor- Bb, C, Db, Eb, F, Gb, Ab, Bb
B Minor- B, C#, D, E, F#, G, A, B

Minor Scales (Harmonic) Method (2, 1, 2, 2, 1, 3, 1)

C Minor- C, D, Eb, F, G, Ab, B, C
C# Minor- C#, D#, E, F#, G#, A, B#, C#
D Minor- D, E, F, G, A, Bb, C#, D
D# Minor- D#, E#, F#, G#, A#, B, Cx, D#
Eb Minor- Eb, F, Gb, Ab, Bb, Cb, D, Eb
E Minor- E, F#, G, A, B, C, D#, E
F Minor- F, G, Ab, Bb, C, Db, E, F
F# Minor- F#, G#, A, B, C#, D, E#, F#
G Minor- G, A, Bb, C, D, Eb, F#, G
G# Minor- G#, A#, B, C#, D#, E, Fx, G#
Ab Minor- Ab, Bb, Cb, Db, Eb, Fb, G, Ab
A Minor- A, B, C, D, E, F, G#, A
A# Minor- A#, B#, C#, D#, E#, F#, Gx, A#

Bb Minor- Bb, C, Db, Eb, F, Gb, A, Bb
B Minor- B, C#, D, E, F#, G, A#, B

Minor Scales (Melodic) Method (2, 1, 2, 2, 2, 2, 1)

C Minor- C, D, Eb, F, G, A, B, C
C# Minor- C#, D#, E, F#, G#, A#, B#, C#
D Minor- D, E, F, G, A, B, C#, D
D# Minor- D#, E#, F#, G#, A#, B#, Cx, D#
Eb Minor- Eb, F, Gb, Ab, Bb, C, D, Eb
E Minor- E, F#, G, A, B, C#, D#, E
F Minor- F, G, Ab, Bb, C, D, E, F
F# Minor- F#, G#, A, B, C#, D#, E#, F#
G Minor- G, A, Bb, C, D, E, F#, G
G# Minor- G#, A#, B, C#, D#, E#, Fx, G#
Ab Minor- Ab, Bb, Cb, Db, Eb, F, G, Ab
A Minor- A, B, C, D, E, F#, G#, A
A# Minor- A#, B#, C#, D#, E#, Fx, Gx, A#
Bb Minor- Bb, C, Db, Eb, F, G, A, Bb
B Minor- B, C#, D, E, F#, G#, A#, B

A SMALL LIST OF MUSICAL SCALES

Arabian
C D E F Gb Ab Bb C

Augmented
C D# E G Ab B C

Bebop
C D E F G A
Bb B C

Blues Scale
C Eb F F# G Bb C

Blues Scale (chromatic)
C D Eb E F F# G A
Bb C

Blues Scale with additional tones
C D Eb E F F# G A Bb B C

Byzantine (same as
Gypsy Minor)
C Db E F G Ab B C

Chinese (Major Pentatonic)
C D E G A
C

Chromatic
C C# D D# E F F# G G# A A# B C

Diminished (8 tones, begins with
HALF
step)
C Db D# E F# G A Bb C

Diminished (8 tones, begins with
WHOLE
step)
C D Eb F Gb Ab A B C

Diminished Whole Tone (Alternate)
(has b9, #9,
#4, #5, b7)
C Db D# E F# G# Bb C

Dominant 7th (Mixolydian)(Major with b7)
C D E F G A
Bb C

Dominant 7th SUS 4
C D F G A Bb C

Ethiopian
C D Eb F G Ab Bb

Half-Diminished (Locrian)
(Same as Major □ step up)
C Db Eb F Gb Ab Bb C

Gypsy Minor (Byzantine)
C Db E F G Ab B C C Half-Diminished #2
(2nd tone raised by a half step)
C D Eb F Gb Ab Bb C

Harmonic Major
C D E F G Ab B C

Harmonic
Minor
C D Eb F G Ab B C

Hawaiian
C D Eb G A C

Hindu (Dominant 7th with
b6)
C D E F G Ab Bb C

Hungarian
C D# E F# G A Bb C

Hungarian Gypsy
C D
Eb F# G Ab B C

In Sen (Japanese)
C C# F G Bb

Japanese (A)
C Db F G Ab
C

Japanese (B)
C D F G Ab C

Javanese
C Db Eb F G A Bb C

Jewish Scale
(same as Spanish)
C Db E F G Ab Bb C

Lydian (Major with #4)
C D E F# G A B C

Lydian Augmented (Major with #4 & #5)
C D E F# G# A B C

Lydian Dominant
(Dominant 7th with #4)
C D E F# G A Bb C

Major (Ionian)
C D E F G A B C

Major
Bebop
C D E F G G# A B C

Major Pentatonic (5 tone scale)
C D E G A C

Minor
(Dorian)(Major with b3 and b7)
C D Eb F G A Bb C

Minor (harmonic)(has b3 and b6)
C D Eb F G Ab B C

Minor
(melodic, ascending)(Jazz Minor)
C D Eb F G A B C

Minor (Phrygian)
C Db Eb F G Ab Bb
C

Minor (Pure, Natural, Aeolian)
C D Eb F G Ab Bb C

Minor Bebop
C D Eb E F G
A Bb C

Minor Pentatonic
C D Eb G A C

Mohammedan (same as pure minor)
C D Eb
F G Ab Bb C

Mongolian (Major Pentatonic)
C D E G A C

Neopolitan
C Db Eb F G
Ab B C

Oriental
C Db E F Gb Ab Bb C

Pentatonic (?)
C D F G A
C

Persian
C Db E F Gb Ab B C

Phrygian
C Db Eb F G Ab Bb C

Spanish
(Jewish)
C Db E F G Ab Bb C

Whole Tone (Dominant 7th with #4, #5)
C D E F# G# Bb C

A SMALL LIST OF MUSICAL SCALES

Arabian
C D E F Gb Ab Bb C

Augmented
C D# E G Ab B C

Bebop
C D E F G A
Bb B C

Blues Scale
C Eb F F# G Bb C

Blues Scale (chromatic)
C D Eb E F F# G A
Bb C

Blues Scale with additional tones
C D Eb E F F# G A Bb B C

Byzantine (same as
Gypsy Minor)
C Db E F G Ab B C

Chinese (Major Pentatonic)
C D E G A
C

Chromatic
C C# D D# E F F# G G# A A# B C

Diminished (8 tones, begins with
HALF
step)
C Db D# E F# G A Bb C

Diminished (8 tones, begins with
WHOLE
step)
C D Eb F Gb Ab A B C

Diminished Whole Tone (Alternate)
(has b9, #9,
#4, #5, b7)
C Db D# E F# G# Bb C

Dominant 7th (Mixolydian)(Major with b7)
C D E F G A
Bb C

Dominant 7th SUS 4
C D F G A Bb C

Ethiopian
C D Eb F G Ab Bb

Half-Diminished (Locrian)
(Same as Major □ step up)
C Db Eb F Gb Ab Bb C

Gypsy Minor (Byzantine)
C Db E F G Ab B C C Half-Diminished #2
(2nd tone raised by a half step)
C D Eb F Gb Ab Bb C

Harmonic Major
C D E F G Ab B C

Harmonic
Minor
C D Eb F G Ab B C

Hawaiian
C D Eb G A C

Hindu (Dominant 7th with
b6)
C D E F G Ab Bb C

Hungarian
C D# E F# G A Bb C

Hungarian Gypsy
C D
Eb F# G Ab B C

In Sen (Japanese)
C C# F G Bb

Japanese (A)
C Db F G Ab
C

Japanese (B)
C D F G Ab C

Javanese
C Db Eb F G A Bb C

Jewish Scale
(same as Spanish)
C Db E F G Ab Bb C

Lydian (Major with #4)
C D E F# G A B
C

Lydian Augmented (Major with #4 & #5)
C D E F# G# A B C

Lydian Dominant
(Dominant 7th with #4)
C D E F# G A Bb C

Major (Ionian)
C D E F G A B C

Major
Bebop
C D E F G G# A B C Major Pentatonic (5 tone scale)
C D E G A C

Minor
(Dorian)(Major with b3 and b7)
C D Eb F G A Bb C

Minor (harmonic)(has b3 and b6)
C D Eb F G Ab B C

Minor
(melodic, ascending)(Jazz Minor)
C D Eb F G A B C

Minor (Phrygian)
C Db Eb F G Ab Bb
C

Minor (Pure, Natural, Aeolian)
C D Eb F G Ab Bb C

Minor Bebop
C D Eb E F G
A Bb C

Minor Pentatonic
C D Eb G A C

Mohammedan (same as pure minor)
C D Eb
F G Ab Bb C

Mongolian (Major Pentatonic)
C D E G A C

Neopolitan
C Db Eb F G
Ab B C

Oriental
C Db E F Gb Ab Bb C

Pentatonic (?)
C D F G A
C

Persian
C Db E F Gb Ab B C

Phrygian
C Db Eb F G Ab Bb C

Spanish
(Jewish)
C Db E F G Ab Bb C

Whole Tone (Dominant 7th with #4, #5)
C D E F# G# Bb C

Using key of A Major:

1. A - Ionian

2. B - Dorian

3. C# - Phrygian

4. D - Lydian

5. E - Mixolydian

6. F# - AeoliańF# Minor

7. G# - Locrian

Using key of A# or B Flat Major:

1. B Flat - Ionian

2. C - Dorian

3. D - Phrygian

4. D# - Lydian

5. F - Mixolydian

6. G - AeoliańG Minor

7. A - Locrian

Using key of B Major:

1. B - Ionian

2. C# - Dorian

3. D# - Phrygian

4. E - Lydian

5. F# - Mixolydian

6. G# - AeolianǴG# Minor

7. A# - Locrian

using key C Major:

1. C - Ionian

2. D - Dorian

3. E - Phrygian

4. F - Lydian

5. G - Mixolydian

6. A - AeolianÁA Minor

7. B - Locrian

Using key of C# or D Flat Major:

1. C# - Ionian

2. D# - Dorian

3. F - Phrygian

4. F# - Lydian

5. G# - Mixolydian

6. B Flat - AeoliańB Flat Minor

7. C - Locrian

Using key of D Major:

1. D - Ionian

2. E - Dorian

3. F# - Phrygian

4. G - Lydian

5. A - Mixolydian

6. B - AeoliańB Minor

7. C# - Locrian

Using key of D# or E Flat Major:

1. D# - Ionian

2. F - Dorian

3. G - Phrygian

4. G# - Lydian

5. B Flat - Mixolydian

6. C - AeolianćC Minor

7. D - Locrian

Using key of E Major:

1. E - Ionian

2. F# - Dorian

3. G# - Phrygian

4. A - Lydian

5. B - Mixolydian

6. C# - AeolianćC# Minor

7. D# - Locrian

Using key of F Major:

1. F - Ionian
2. G - Dorian
3. A - Phrygian
4. A# - Lydian
5. C - Mixolydian
6. D - AeoliańD Minor
7. E - Locrian

Using key of F# or G Flat Major:

1. F# - Ionian
2. G# - Dorian
3. A# - Phrygian
4. B - Lydian
5. C# - Mixolydian
6. D# - AeoliańD# Minor
7. F - Locrian

Using key of G Major:

1. G - Ionian

2. A - Dorian

3. B - Phrygian

4. C - Lydian

5. D - Mixolydian

6. E - AeolianńE Minor

7. F# - Locrian

Using key of G# or A Flat Major:

1. G# - Ionian

2. A# - Dorian

3. C - Phrygian

4. C# - Lydian

5. D# - Mixolydian

6. F - AeolianńF Minor

7. G - Locrian

rootModes Scale

1. A Ionian A Major
2. A Dorian G Major
3. A Phrygian F Major
4. A Lydian E Major
5. A Mixolydian D Major
6. A Aeolian A Minor C Major
7. A Locrian B Flat

1. A#B Flat Ionian A# Flat Major
2. A#B Flat Dorian G# Major
3. A#B Flat Phrygian F# Major
4. A#B Flat Lydian F Major
5. A#B Flat Mixolydian D# Major
6. A#B Flat Aeolian A# Minor C# Major
7. A#B Flat Locrian B Major

1. B Ionian B Major
2. B Dorian A Major
3. B Phrygian G Major
4. B Lydian F# Major
5. B Mixolydian E Major
6. B Aeolian B Minor D Major
7. B Locrian C Major

1. C Ionianˆ C Major
2. C Dorianˆ A# Major
3. C Phrygianˆ G# Major
4. C Lydianˆ G Major
5. C Mixolydianˆ F Major
6. C Aeolian´C Minorˆ D# Major
7. C Locrianˆ C# Major

1. C# Ionianˆ C# Major
2. C# Dorianˆ B Major
3. C# Phrygianˆ A Major
4. C# Lydianˆ G# Major
5. C# Mixolydianˆ F# Major
6. C# Aeolian´C# Minorˆ E Major
7. C# Locrianˆ D Major

1. D Ionianˆ D Major
2. D Dorianˆ C Major
3. D Phrygianˆ A# Major
4. D Lydianˆ A Major
5. D Mixolydianˆ G Major
6. D Aeolian´D Minorˆ F Major
7. D Locrianˆ D# Major

1. D# Ionianˆ D# Major
2. D# Dorianˆ C# Major
3. D# Phrygianˆ B Major
4. D# Lydianˆ A# Major
5. D# Mixolydianˆ G# Major
6. D# Aeolian´D# Minorˆ F# Major
7. D# Locrianˆ E Major

1. E Ionian̂ E Major
2. E Dorian̂ D Major
3. E Phrygian̂ C Major
4. E Lydian̂ B Major
5. E Mixolydian̂ A Major
6. E AeoliańE Minor̂ G Major
7. E Locrian̂ F Major

1. F Ionian̂ F Major
2. F Dorian̂ D# Major
3. F Phrygian̂ C# Major
4. F Lydian̂ C Major
5. F Mixolydian̂ A# Major
6. F AeoliańF Minor̂ G# Major
7. F Locrian̂ F# Major

1. F# Ionian̂ F# Major
2. F# Dorian̂ E Major
3. F# Phrygian̂ D Major
4. F# Lydian̂ C# Major
5. F# Mixolydian̂ B Major
6. F# AeoliańF# Minor̂ A Major
7. F# Locrian̂ G Major

1. G Ionian̂ G Major
2. G Dorian̂ F Major
3. G Phrygian̂ D# Major
4. G Lydian̂ D Major
5. G Mixolydian̂ C Major
6. G AeoliańG Minor̂ A# Major
7. G Locrian̂ G# Major

1. G# Ionian̂ G# Major
2. G# Dorian̂ F# Major
3. G# Phrygian̂ E Major
4. G# Lydian̂ D# Major
5. G# Mixolydian̂ C# Major
6. G# AeoliańG# Minor̂ B Major
7. G# Locrian̂ A Major

Lydian Hexatonic
C,D,E,G,A,B
G,A,B,D,E,^F
D,E,^F,A,B,^C
A,B,^C,E,^F,^G
E,^F,^G,B,^C,^D
B,^C,^D,^F,^G,^A
^F,^G,^A,^C,^D,^E
F,G,A,C,D,E
Bb,C,D,F,G,A
Eb,F,G,Bb,C,D
Ab,Bb,C,Eb,F,G
Db,Eb,F,Ab,Bb,C
Gb,Ab,Bb,Db,Eb,F

Mixolydian Hexatonic
C,D,F,G,A,Bb
G,A,C,D,E,F
D,E,G,A,B,C
A,B,D,E,^F,G
E,^F,A,B,^C,D
B,^C,E,^F,^G,A
^F,^G,B,^C,^D,E
F,G,Bb,C,D,Eb
Bb,C,Eb,F,G,Ab
Eb,F,Ab,Bb,C,Db
Ab,Bb,Db,Eb,F,Gb
Db,Eb,Gb,Ab,Bb,Cb
Gb,Ab,Cb,Db,Eb,Fb

Phrygian Hexatonic
C,Eb,F,G,Ab,Bb
G,Bb,C,D,Eb,F
D,F,G,A,Bb,C
A,C,D,E,F,G
E,G,A,B,C,D
B,D,E,^F,G,A
^F,A,B,^C,D,E
F,Ab,Bb,C,Db,Eb
Bb,Db,Eb,F,Gb,Ab
Eb,Gb,Ab,Bb,Cb,Db
Ab,Cb,Db,Eb,Fb,Gb
Db,Fb,Gb,Ab,Bbb,Cb
Gb,Bbb,Cb,Db,Ebb,Fb

Phrygian Tetrachord
C,Db,Eb,F
G,Ab,Bb,C
D,Eb,F,G
A,Bb,C,D
E,F,G,A
B,C,D,E
^F,G,A,B
F,Gb,Ab,Bb
Bb,Cb,Db,Eb
Eb,Fb,Gb,Ab
Ab,Bbb,Cb,Db
Db,Ebb,Fb,Gb
Gb,Abb,Bbb,Cb

Phrygian Trichord
C,Db,Eb
G,Ab,Bb
D,Eb,F
A,Bb,C
E,F,G
B,C,D
^F,G,A
F,Gb,Ab
Bb,Cb,Db
Eb,Fb,Gb
Ab,Bbb,Cb
Db,Ebb,Fb
Gb,Abb,Bbb

Dorian Tetrachord
C,D,Eb,F
G,A,Bb,C
D,E,F,G
A,B,C,D
E,^F,G,A
B,^C,D,E
^F,^G,A,B
F,G,Ab,Bb
Bb,C,Db,Eb
Eb,F,Gb,Ab
Ab,Bb,Cb,Db
Db,Eb,Fb,Gb
Gb,Ab,Bbb,Cb

Lydian, Kalyan F,to E,ascendinG,naturals
C,D,E,^F,G,A,B
G,A,B,^C,D,E,^F
D,E,^F,^G,A,B,^C
A,B,^C,^D,E,^F,^G
E,^F,^G,^A,B,^C,^D
B,^C,^D,^E,^F,^G,^A
^F,^G,^A,^B,^C,^D,^E
F,G,A,B,C,D,E
Bb,C,D,E,F,G,A
Eb,F,G,A,Bb,C,D
Ab,Bb,C,D,Eb,F,G
Db,Eb,F,G,Ab,Bb,C
Gb,Ab,Bb,C,Db,Eb,F

Ionian, Major, Bilaval C,to B,asc. nats.
C,D,E,F,G,A,B
G,A,B,C,D,E,^F
D,E,^F,G,A,B,^C
A,B,^C,D,E,^F,^G
E,^F,^G,A,B,^C,^D
B,^C,^D,E,^F,^G,^A
^F,^G,^A,B,^C,^D,^E
F,G,A,Bb,C,D,E
Bb,C,D,Eb,F,G,A
Eb,F,G,Ab,Bb,C,D
Ab,Bb,C,Db,Eb,F,G
Db,Eb,F,Gb,Ab,Bb,C
Gb,Ab,Bb,Cb,Db,Eb,F

Mixolydian, Khamaj G,to F,ascend. nats
C,D,E,F,G,A,Bb
G,A,B,C,D,E,F
D,E,^F,G,A,B,C
A,B,^C,D,E,^F,G
E,^F,^G,A,B,^C,D
B,^C,^D,E,^F,^G,A
^F,^G,^A,B,^C,^D,E
F,G,A,Bb,C,D,Eb
Bb,C,D,Eb,F,G,Ab
Eb,F,G,Ab,Bb,C,Db
Ab,Bb,C,Db,Eb,F,Gb
Db,Eb,F,Gb,Ab,Bb,Cb
Gb,Ab,Bb,Cb,Db,Eb,Fb

Dorian, Kafi D,to C,asc. naturals
C,D,Eb,F,G,A,Bb
G,A,Bb,C,D,E,F
D,E,F,G,A,B,C
A,B,C,D,E,^F,G
E,^F,G,A,B,^C,D
B,^C,D,E,^F,^G,A
^F,^G,A,B,^C,^D,E
F,G,Ab,Bb,C,D,Eb
Bb,C,Db,Eb,F,G,Ab
Eb,F,Gb,Ab,Bb,C,Db
Ab,Bb,Cb,Db,Eb,F,Gb
Db,Eb,Fb,Gb,Ab,Bb,Cb
Gb,Ab,Bbb,Cb,Db,Eb,Fb

Aeolian Natural Minor, Asavari AsC,Nats. A,to G
C,D,Eb,F,G,Ab,Bb
G,A,Bb,C,D,Eb,F
D,E,F,G,A,Bb,C
A,B,C,D,E,F,G
E,^F,G,A,B,C,D
B,^C,D,E,^F,G,A
^F,^G,A,B,^C,D,E
F,G,Ab,Bb,C,Db,Eb
Bb,C,Db,Eb,F,Gb,Ab
Eb,F,Gb,Ab,Bb,Cb,Db
Ab,Bb,Cb,Db,Eb,Fb,Gb
Db,Eb,Fb,Gb,Ab,Bbb,Cb
Gb,Ab,Bbb,Cb,Db,Ebb,Fb

Phrygian, Bhairavi E,to D,asc. nats.(as 11́678910́4 in 12edo)
C,Db,Eb,F,G,Ab,Bb
G,Ab,Bb,C,D,Eb,F
D,Eb,F,G,A,Bb,C
A,Bb,C,D,E,F,G
E,F,G,A,B,C,D
B,C,D,E,^F,G,A
^F,G,A,B,^C,D,E
F,Gb,Ab,Bb,C,Db,Eb
Bb,Cb,Db,Eb,F,Gb,Ab
Eb,Fb,Gb,Ab,Bb,Cb,Db
Ab,Bbb,Cb,Db,Eb,Fb,Gb
Db,Ebb,Fb,Gb,Ab,Bbb,Cb
Gb,Abb,Bbb,Cb,Db,Ebb,Fb

Locrian û B,to A,AscendinG,naturals
C,Db,Eb,F,Gb,Ab,Bb
G,Ab,Bb,C,Db,Eb,F
D,Eb,F,G,Ab,Bb,C
A,Bb,C,D,Eb,F,G
E,F,G,A,Bb,C,D
B,C,D,E,F,G,A
^F,G,A,B,C,D,E
F,Gb,Ab,Bb,Cb,Db,Eb
Bb,Cb,Db,Eb,Fb,Gb,Ab
Eb,Fb,Gb,Ab,Bbb,Cb,Db
Ab,Bbb,Cb,Db,Ebb,Fb,Gb
Db,Ebb,Fb,Gb,Abb,Bbb,Cb
Gb,Abb,Bbb,Cb,Dbb,Ebb,Fb

Lydian, Kalyan F,to E,ascendinG,naturals
C,D,E,^F,G,A,B
G,A,B,^C,D,E,^F
D,E,^F,^G,A,B,^C
A,B,^C,^D,E,^F,^G
E,^F,^G,^A,B,^C,^D
B,^C,^D,^E,^F,^G,^A
^F,^G,^A,^B,^C,^D,^E
F,G,A,B,C,D,E
Bb,C,D,E,F,G,A
Eb,F,G,A,Bb,C,D
Ab,Bb,C,D,Eb,F,G
Db,Eb,F,G,Ab,Bb,C
Gb,Ab,Bb,C,Db,Eb,F

Ionian, Major, Bilaval C,to B,asc. nats.
C,D,E,F,G,A,B
G,A,B,C,D,E,^F
D,E,^F,G,A,B,^C
A,B,^C,D,E,^F,^G
E,^F,^G,A,B,^C,^D
B,^C,^D,E,^F,^G,^A
^F,^G,^A,B,^C,^D,^E
F,G,A,Bb,C,D,E
Bb,C,D,Eb,F,G,A
Eb,F,G,Ab,Bb,C,D
Ab,Bb,C,Db,Eb,F,G
Db,Eb,F,Gb,Ab,Bb,C
Gb,Ab,Bb,Cb,Db,Eb,F

Mixolydian, Khamaj G,to F,ascend. nats
C,D,E,F,G,A,Bb
G,A,B,C,D,E,F
D,E,^F,G,A,B,C
A,B,^C,D,E,^F,G
E,^F,^G,A,B,^C,D
B,^C,^D,E,^F,^G,A
^F,^G,^A,B,^C,^D,E
F,G,A,Bb,C,D,Eb
Bb,C,D,Eb,F,G,Ab
Eb,F,G,Ab,Bb,C,Db
Ab,Bb,C,Db,Eb,F,Gb
Db,Eb,F,Gb,Ab,Bb,Cb
Gb,Ab,Bb,Cb,Db,Eb,Fb

Dorian, Kafi D,to C,asc. naturals
C,D,Eb,F,G,A,Bb
G,A,Bb,C,D,E,F
D,E,F,G,A,B,C
A,B,C,D,E,^F,G
E,^F,G,A,B,^C,D
B,^C,D,E,^F,^G,A
^F,^G,A,B,^C,^D,E
F,G,Ab,Bb,C,D,Eb
Bb,C,Db,Eb,F,G,Ab
Eb,F,Gb,Ab,Bb,C,Db
Ab,Bb,Cb,Db,Eb,F,Gb
Db,Eb,Fb,Gb,Ab,Bb,Cb
Gb,Ab,Bbb,Cb,Db,Eb,Fb

Aeolian Natural Minor, Asavari AsC,Nats. A,to G
C,D,Eb,F,G,Ab,Bb
G,A,Bb,C,D,Eb,F
D,E,F,G,A,Bb,C
A,B,C,D,E,F,G
E,^F,G,A,B,C,D
B,^C,D,E,^F,G,A
^F,^G,A,B,^C,D,E
F,G,Ab,Bb,C,Db,Eb
Bb,C,Db,Eb,F,Gb,Ab
Eb,F,Gb,Ab,Bb,Cb,Db
Ab,Bb,Cb,Db,Eb,Fb,Gb
Db,Eb,Fb,Gb,Ab,Bbb,Cb
Gb,Ab,Bbb,Cb,Db,Ebb,Fb

Phrygian, Bhairavi E,to D,asc. nats.(as 11́67891 0́4 in 12edo)
C,Db,Eb,F,G,Ab,Bb
G,Ab,Bb,C,D,Eb,F
D,Eb,F,G,A,Bb,C
A,Bb,C,D,E,F,G
E,F,G,A,B,C,D
B,C,D,E,^F,G,A
^F,G,A,B,^C,D,E
F,Gb,Ab,Bb,C,Db,Eb
Bb,Cb,Db,Eb,F,Gb,Ab
Eb,Fb,Gb,Ab,Bb,Cb,Db
Ab,Bbb,Cb,Db,Eb,Fb,Gb
Db,Ebb,Fb,Gb,Ab,Bbb,Cb
Gb,Abb,Bbb,Cb,Db,Ebb,Fb

Locrian û B,to A,AscendinG,naturals
C,Db,Eb,F,Gb,Ab,Bb
G,Ab,Bb,C,Db,Eb,F
D,Eb,F,G,Ab,Bb,C
A,Bb,C,D,Eb,F,G
E,F,G,A,Bb,C,D
B,C,D,E,F,G,A
^F,G,A,B,C,D,E
F,Gb,Ab,Bb,Cb,Db,Eb
Bb,Cb,Db,Eb,Fb,Gb,Ab
Eb,Fb,Gb,Ab,Bbb,Cb,Db
Ab,Bbb,Cb,Db,Ebb,Fb,Gb
Db,Ebb,Fb,Gb,Abb,Bbb,Cb
Gb,Abb,Bbb,Cb,Dbb,Ebb,Fb

Locrian PentaMirror
C,Db,Eb,F,Gb
G,Ab,Bb,C,Db
D,Eb,F,G,Ab
A,Bb,C,D,Eb
E,F,G,A,Bb
B,C,D,E,F
^F,G,A,B,C
F,Gb,Ab,Bb,Cb
Bb,Cb,Db,Eb,Fb
Eb,Fb,Gb,Ab,Bbb
Ab,Bbb,Cb,Db,Ebb
Db,Ebb,Fb,Gb,Abb
Gb,Abb,Bbb,Cb,Dbb

Ionian PentatoniC,RagA,GambhiranatA,(India)
C,E,F,G,B
G,B,C,D,^F
D,^F,G,A,^C
A,^C,D,E,^G
E,^G,A,B,^D
B,^D,E,^F,^A
^F,^A,B,^C,^E
F,A,Bb,C,E
Bb,D,Eb,F,A
Eb,G,Ab,Bb,D
Ab,C,Db,Eb,G
Db,F,Gb,Ab,C
Gb,Bb,Cb,Db,F

Lydian Pentachord
C,D,E,^F,G
G,A,B,^C,D
D,E,^F,^G,A
A,B,^C,^D,E
E,^F,^G,^A,B
B,^C,^D,^E,^F
^F,^G,^A,^B,^C
F,G,A,B,C
Bb,C,D,E,F
Eb,F,G,A,Bb
Ab,Bb,C,D,Eb
Db,Eb,F,G,Ab
Gb,Ab,Bb,C,Db

Mixolydian Pentatonic
C,E,F,G,Bb
G,B,C,D,F
D,^F,G,A,C
A,^C,D,E,G
E,^G,A,B,D
B,^D,E,^F,A
^F,^A,B,^C,E
F,A,Bb,C,Eb
Bb,D,Eb,F,Ab
Eb,G,Ab,Bb,Db
Ab,C,Db,Eb,Gb
Db,F,Gb,Ab,Cb
Gb,Bb,Cb,Db,Fb

Major Lydian Genus Diatonicum Veterum Correctum
C,D,E,F,^F,G,A,B
G,A,B,C,^C,D,E,^F
D,E,^F,G,^G,A,B,^C
A,B,^C,D,^D,E,^F,^G
E,^F,^G,A,^A,B,^C,^D
B,^C,^D,E,^E,^F,^G,^A
^F,^G,^A,B,^B,^C,^D,^E
F,G,A,Bb,B,C,D,E
Bb,C,D,Eb,E,F,G,A
Eb,F,G,Ab,A,Bb,C,D
Ab,Bb,C,Db,D,Eb,F,G
Db,Eb,F,Gb,G,Ab,Bb,C
Gb,Ab,Bb,Cb,C,Db,Eb,F

Dorian Aoelian (Al b-s) 11́891011́4 in 12edo)
C,D,Eb,F,G,Ab,A,Bb
G,A,Bb,C,D,Eb,E,F
D,E,F,G,A,Bb,B,C
A,B,C,D,E,F,^F,G
E,^F,G,A,B,C,^C,D
B,^C,D,E,^F,G,^G,A
^F,^G,A,B,^C,D,^D,E
F,G,Ab,Bb,C,Db,D,Eb
Bb,C,Db,Eb,F,Gb,G,Ab
Eb,F,Gb,Ab,Bb,Cb,C,Db
Ab,Bb,Cb,Db,Eb,Fb,F,Gb
Db,Eb,Fb,Gb,Ab,Bbb,Bb,Cb
Gb,Ab,Bbb,Cb,Db,Ebb,Eb,Fb

Phrygian Aeolian 4b
C,Db,D,Eb,F,G,Ab,Bb
G,Ab,A,Bb,C,D,Eb,F
D,Eb,E,F,G,A,Bb,C
A,Bb,B,C,D,E,F,G
E,F,^F,G,A,B,C,D
B,C,^C,D,E,^F,G,A
^F,G,^G,A,B,^C,D,E
F,Gb,G,Ab,Bb,C,Db,Eb
Bb,Cb,C,Db,Eb,F,Gb,Ab
Eb,Fb,F,Gb,Ab,Bb,Cb,Db
Ab,Bbb,Bb,Cb,Db,Eb,Fb,Gb
Db,Ebb,Eb,Fb,Gb,Ab,Bbb,Cb
Gb,Abb,Ab,Bbb,Cb,Db,Ebb,Fb

Phrygian Locrian (All b-s) û 11́891011́6 in 12edo)
C,Db,Eb,F,Gb,G,Ab,Bb
G,Ab,Bb,C,Db,D,Eb,F
D,Eb,F,G,Ab,A,Bb,C
A,Bb,C,D,Eb,E,F,G
E,F,G,A,Bb,B,C,D
B,C,D,E,F,^F,G,A
^F,G,A,B,C,^C,D,E
F,Gb,Ab,Bb,Cb,C,Db,Eb
Bb,Cb,Db,Eb,Fb,F,Gb,Ab
Eb,Fb,Gb,Ab,Bbb,Bb,Cb,Db
Ab,Bbb,Cb,Db,Ebb,Eb,Fb,Gb
Db,Ebb,Fb,Gb,Abb,Ab,Bbb,Cb
Gb,Abb,Bbb,Cb,Dbb,Db,Ebb,Fb

Blues Dorian Hex (all b-s) as 9́6789́1 in 12edo)
C,D,Eb,E,G,A
G,A,Bb,B,D,E
D,E,F,^F,A,B
A,B,C,^C,E,^F
E,^F,G,^G,B,^C
B,^C,D,^D,^F,^G
^F,^G,A,^A,^C,^D
F,G,Ab,A,C,D
Bb,C,Db,D,F,G
Eb,F,Gb,G,Bb,C
Ab,Bb,Cb,C,Eb,F
Db,Eb,Fb,F,Ab,Bb
Gb,Ab,Bbb,Bb,Db,Eb

Blues Phrygian 11́2891011́6 in 12edo)
C,Db,Eb,F,Gb,G,Bb
G,Ab,Bb,C,Db,D,F
D,Eb,F,G,Ab,A,C
A,Bb,C,D,Eb,E,G
E,F,G,A,Bb,B,D
B,C,D,E,F,^F,A
^F,G,A,B,C,^C,E
F,Gb,Ab,Bb,Cb,C,Eb
Bb,Cb,Db,Eb,Fb,F,Ab
Eb,Fb,Gb,Ab,Bbb,Bb,Db
Ab,Bbb,Cb,Db,Ebb,Eb,Gb
Db,Ebb,Fb,Gb,ABb,Ab,Cb
Gb,Abb,Bbb,Cb,Dbb,Db,Fb

Lydian Mixolydian Taishikicho, Ryo (Japan)
C,D,E,F,^F,G,A,Bb,B
G,A,B,C,^C,D,E,F,^F
D,E,^F,G,^G,A,B,C,^C
A,B,^C,D,^D,E,^F,G,^G
E,^F,^G,A,^A,B,^C,D,^D
B,^C,^D,E,^E,^F,^G,A,^A
^F,^G,^A,B,^B,^C,^D,E,^E
F,G,A,Bb,B,C,D,Eb,E
Bb,C,D,Eb,E,F,G,Ab,A
Eb,F,G,Ab,A,Bb,C,Db,D
Ab,Bb,C,Db,D,Eb,F,Gb,G
Db,Eb,F,Gb,G,Ab,Bb,Cb,C
Gb,Ab,Bb,Cb,C,Db,Eb,Fb,F

ChromatiC,DiatoniC,Dorian (all b)
C,Db,D,Eb,F,G,Ab,A,Bb
G,Ab,A,Bb,C,D,Eb,E,F
D,Eb,E,F,G,A,Bb,B,C
A,Bb,B,C,D,E,F,^F,G
E,F,^F,G,A,B,C,^C,D
B,C,^C,D,E,^F,G,^G,A
^F,G,^G,A,B,^C,D,^D,E
F,Gb,G,Ab,Bb,C,Db,D,Eb
Bb,Cb,C,Db,Eb,F,Gb,G,Ab
Eb,Fb,F,Gb,Ab,Bb,Cb,C,Db
Ab,Bbb,Bb,Cb,Db,Eb,Fb,F,Gb
Db,Ebb,Eb,Fb,Gb,Ab,Bbb,Bb,Cb
Gb,Abb,Ab,Bbb,Cb,Db,Ebb,Eb,Fb

Lydian b3 Hexatonic
C,Eb,E,G,A,B
G,Bb,B,D,E,^F
D,F,^F,A,B,^C
A,C,^C,E,^F,^G
E,G,^G,B,^C,^D
B,D,^D,^F,^G,^A
^F,A,^A,^C,^D,^E
F,Ab,A,C,D,E
Bb,Db,D,F,G,A
Eb,Gb,G,Bb,C,D
Ab,Cb,C,Eb,F,G
Db,Fb,F,Ab,Bb,C
Gb,Bbb,Bb,Db,Eb,F

Prometheus ^F,anD,Bb) in 12edo)
C,D,E,^F,A,Bb
G,A,B,^C,E,F
D,E,^F,^G,B,C
A,B,^C,^D,^F,G
E,^F,^G,^A,^C,D
B,^C,^D,^E,^G,A
^F,^G,^A,^B,^D,E
F,G,A,B,D,Eb
Bb,C,D,E,G,Ab
Eb,F,G,A,C,Db
Ab,Bb,C,D,F,Gb
Db,Eb,F,G,Bb,Cb
Gb,Ab,Bb,C,Eb,Fb

Lydian Augmented, Hindi ^IV & ^V
C,D,E,^F,^G,A,B
G,A,B,^C,^D,E,^F
D,E,^F,^G,^A,B,^C
A,B,^C,^D,^E,^F,^G
E,^F,^G,^A,^B,^C,^D
B,^C,^D,^E,^F^ ^G,^A
^F,^G,^A,^B,^C^ ^D,^E
F,G,A,B,^C,D,E
Bb,C,D,E,^F,G,A
Eb,F,G,A,B,C,D
Ab,Bb,C,D,E,F,G
Db,Eb,F,G,A,Bb,C
Gb,Ab,Bb,C,D,Eb,F

Lydian Dominant, Overtone, Hindi ^IV & bVII
C,D,E,^F,G,A,Bb
G,A,B,^C,D,E,F
D,E,^F,^G,A,B,C
A,B,^C,^D,E,^F,G
E,^F,^G,^A,B,^C,D
B,^C,^D,^E,^F,^G,A
^F,^G,^A,^B,^C,^D,E
F,G,A,B,C,D,Eb
Bb,C,D,E,F,G,Ab
Eb,F,G,A,Bb,C,Db
Ab,Bb,C,D,Eb,F,Gb
Db,Eb,F,G,Ab,Bb,Cb
Gb,Ab,Bb,C,Db,Eb,Fb

Minor Locrian, Hindi 3 flats anD,bV
C,D,Eb,F,Gb,Ab,Bb
G,A,Bb,C,Db,Eb,F
D,E,F,G,Ab,Bb,C
A,B,C,D,Eb,F,G
E,^F,G,A,Bb,C,D
B,^C,D,E,F,G,A
^F,^G,A,B,C,D,E
F,G,Ab,Bb,Cb,Db,Eb
Bb,C,Db,Eb,Fb,Gb,Ab
Eb,F,Gb,Ab,Bbb,Cb,Db
Ab,Bb,Cb,Db,Ebb,Fb,Gb
Db,Eb,Fb,Gb,Abb,Bbb,Cb
Gb,Ab,Bbb,Cb,DBb,Ebb,Fb

ChromatiC,Hypodorian
C,D,Eb,E,G,Ab,A
G,A,Bb,B,D,Eb,E
D,E,F,^F,A,Bb,B
A,B,C,^C,E,F,^F
E,^F,G,^G,B,C,^C
B,^C,D,^D,^F,G,^G
^F,^G,A,^A,^C,D,^D
F,G,Ab,A,C,Db,D
Bb,C,Db,D,F,Gb,G
Eb,F,Gb,G,Bb,Cb,C
Ab,Bb,Cb,C,Eb,Fb,F
Db,Eb,Fb,F,Ab,Bbb,Bb
Gb,Ab,Bbb,Bb,Db,Ebb,Eb

ChromatiC,Phrygian Inverse
C,^C,D,E,G,^G,A
G,^G,A,B,D,^D,E
D,^D,E,^F,A,^A,B
A,^A,B,^C,E,^E,^F
E,^E,^F,^G,B,^B,^C
B,^B,^C,^D,^F,^F^ ^G
^F,^F^ ^G,^A,^C,^C^ ^D
F,^F,G,A,C,^C,D
Bb,B,C,D,F,^F,G
Eb,E,F,G,Bb,B,C
Ab,A,Bb,C,Eb,E,F
Db,D,Eb,F,Ab,A,Bb
Gb,G,Ab,Bb,Db,D,Eb

ChromatiC,Hypophrygian Inverse
C,^C,D,F,^F,G,A
G,^G,A,C,^C,D,E
D,^D,E,G,^G,A,B
A,^A,B,D,^D,E,^F
E,^E,^F,A,^A,B,^C
B,^B,^C,E,^E,^F,^G
^F,^F^ ^G,B,^B,^C,^D
F,^F,G,Bb,B,C,D
Bb,B,C,Eb,E,F,G
Eb,E,F,Ab,A,Bb,C
Ab,A,Bb,Db,D,Eb,F
Db,D,Eb,Gb,G,Ab,Bb
Gb,G,Ab,Cb,C,Db,Eb

Lydian ^2 Hexatonic
C,^D,E,G,A,B
G,^A,B,D,E,^F
D,^E,^F,A,B,^C
A,^B,^C,E,^F,^G
E,^F^ ^G,B,^C,^D
B,^C^ ^D,^F,^G,^A
^F,^G^ ^A,^C,^D,^E
F,^G,A,C,D,E
Bb,^C,D,F,G,A
Eb,^F,G,Bb,C,D
Ab,B,C,Eb,F,G
Db,E,F,Ab,Bb,C
Gb,A,Bb,Db,Eb,F

Phrygian Dominant, Dorico Flamenco, AvahA,RAba, Spanish Folk, Jewish Major
C,Db,E,F,G,Ab,Bb
G,Ab,B,C,D,Eb,F
D,Eb,^F,G,A,Bb,C
A,Bb,^C,D,E,F,G
E,F,^G,A,B,C,D
B,C,^D,E,^F,G,A
^F,G,^A,B,^C,D,E
F,Gb,A,Bb,C,Db,Eb
Bb,Cb,D,Eb,F,Gb,Ab
Eb,Fb,G,Ab,Bb,Cb,Db
Ab,Bbb,C,Db,Eb,Fb,Gb
Db,Ebb,F,Gb,Ab,Bbb,Cb
Gb,Abb,Bb,Cb,Db,Ebb,Fb

Locrian Bb7
C,Db,Eb,F,Gb,Ab,Bb
G,Ab,Bb,C,Db,Eb,F
D,Eb,F,G,Ab,Bb,C
A,Bb,C,D,Eb,F,G
E,F,G,A,Bb,C,D
B,C,D,E,F,G,A
^F,G,A,B,C,D,E
F,Gb,Ab,Bb,Cb,Db,Eb
Bb,Cb,Db,Eb,Fb,Gb,Ab
Eb,Fb,Gb,Ab,Bbb,Cb,Db
Ab,Bbb,Cb,Db,Ebb,Fb,Gb
Db,Ebb,Fb,Gb,ABb,Bbb,Cb
Gb,ABb,Bbb,Cb,Dbb,Ebb,Fb

Phrygian Major, Flamenco, Spanish Phrygian
C,Db,Eb,Fb,F,G,Ab,Bb
G,Ab,Bb,Cb,C,D,Eb,F
D,Eb,F,Gb,G,A,Bb,C
A,Bb,C,Db,D,E,F,G
E,F,G,Ab,A,B,C,D
B,C,D,Eb,E,^F,G,A
^F,G,A,Bb,B,^C,D,E
F,Gb,Ab,Bbb,Bb,C,Db,Eb
Bb,Cb,Db,Ebb,Eb,F,Gb,Ab
Eb,Fb,Gb,Abb,Ab,Bb,Cb,Db
Ab,Bbb,Cb,Dbb,Db,Eb,Fb,Gb
Db,Ebb,Fb,Gbb,Gb,Ab,Bbb,Cb
Gb,Abb,Bbb,Cbb,Cb,Db,Ebb,Fb

UltrA,Locrian
C,^C,^D,E,^F,^G,A
G,^G,^A,B,^C,^D,E
D,^D,^E,^F,^G,^A,B
A,^A,^B,^C,^D,^E,^F
E,^E,^F^ ^G,^A,^B,^C
B,^B,^C^ ^D,^E,^F^ ^G
^F,^F^ ^G^ ^A,^B,^C^ ^D
F,^F,^G,A,B,^C,D
Bb,B,^C,D,E,^F,G
Eb,E,^F,G,A,B,C
Ab,A,B,C,D,E,F
Db,D,E,F,G,A,Bb
Gb,G,A,Bb,C,D,Eb

Aeolian Sharp 1?
C,^D,E,^F,^G,A,B
G,^A,B,^C,^D,E,^F
D,^E,^F,^G,^A,B,^C
A,^B,^C,^D,^E,^F,^G
E,^F^ ^G,^A,^B,^C,^D
B,^C^ ^D,^E,^F^ ^G,^A
^F,^G^ ^A,^B,^C^ ^D,^E
F,^G,A,B,^C,D,E
Bb,^C,D,E,^F,G,A
Eb,^F,G,A,B,C,D
Ab,B,C,D,E,F,G
Db,E,F,G,A,Bb,C
Gb,A,Bb,C,D,Eb,F

Lydian Diminished
C,D,Eb,^F,G,A,B
G,A,Bb,^C,D,E,^F
D,E,F,^G,A,B,^C
A,B,C,^D,E,^F,^G
E,^F,G,^A,B,^C,^D
B,^C,D,^E,^F,^G,^A
^F,^G,A,^B,^C,^D,^E
F,G,Ab,B,C,D,E
Bb,C,Db,E,F,G,A
Eb,F,Gb,A,Bb,C,D
Ab,Bb,Cb,D,Eb,F,G
Db,Eb,Fb,G,Ab,Bb,C
Gb,Ab,Bbb,C,Db,Eb,F

Dorian b5

C,D,Eb,F,Gb,A,Bb

G,A,Bb,C,Db,E,F

D,E,F,G,Ab,B,C

A,B,C,D,Eb,^F,G

E,^F,G,A,Bb,^C,D

B,^C,D,E,F,^G,A

^F,^G,A,B,C,^D,E

F,G,Ab,Bb,Cb,D,Eb

Bb,C,Db,Eb,Fb,G,Ab

Eb,F,Gb,Ab,Bbb,C,Db

Ab,Bb,Cb,Db,Ebb,F,Gb

Db,Eb,Fb,Gb,Abb,Bb,Cb

Gb,Ab,Bbb,Cb,Dbb,Eb,Fb

Blues Dorian Hexatonic

C,Db,Eb,E,G,A

G,Ab,Bb,B,D,E

D,Eb,F,^F,A,B

A,Bb,C,^C,E,^F

E,F,G,^G,B,^C

B,C,D,^D,^F,^G

^F,G,A,^A,^C,^D

F,Gb,Ab,A,C,D

Bb,Cb,Db,D,F,G

Eb,Fb,Gb,G,Bb,C

Ab,Bbb,Cb,C,Eb,F

Db,Ebb,Fb,F,Ab,Bb

Gb,Abb,Bbb,Bb,Db,Eb

ChromatiC,Mixolydian
C,^C,D,E,^F,G,Bb
G,^G,A,B,^C,D,F
D,^D,E,^F,^G,A,C
A,^A,B,^C,^D,E,G
E,^E,^F,^G,^A,B,D
B,^B,^C,^D,^E,^F,A
^F,^F^ ^G,^A,^B,^C,E
F,^F,G,A,B,C,Eb
Bb,B,C,D,E,F,Ab
Eb,E,F,G,A,Bb,Db
Ab,A,Bb,C,D,Eb,Gb
Db,D,Eb,F,G,Ab,Cb
Gb,G,Ab,Bb,C,Db,Fb

Moorish Phrygian 6 b-s
C,Db,Eb,Fb,F,G,Ab,Bb,Cb
G,Ab,Bb,Cb,C,D,Eb,F,Gb
D,Eb,F,Gb,G,A,Bb,C,Db
A,Bb,C,Db,D,E,F,G,Ab
E,F,G,Ab,A,B,C,D,Eb
B,C,D,Eb,E,^F,G,A,Bb
^F,G,A,Bb,B,^C,D,E,F
F,Gb,Ab,Bbb,Bb,C,Db,Eb,Fb
Bb,Cb,Db,Ebb,Eb,F,Gb,Ab,Bbb
Eb,Fb,Gb,ABb,Ab,Bb,Cb,Db,Ebb
Ab,Bbb,Cb,DBb,Db,Eb,Fb,Gb,Abb
Db,Ebb,Fb,Gbb,Gb,Ab,Bbb,Cb,DBb
Gb,Abb,Bbb,Cbb,Cb,Db,Ebb,Fb,Gbb

Double-Phrygian Hexatonic
C,Db,Eb,F,Gb,A
G,Ab,Bb,C,Db,E
D,Eb,F,G,Ab,B
A,Bb,C,D,Eb,^F
E,F,G,A,Bb,^C
B,C,D,E,F,^G
^F,G,A,B,C,^D
F,Gb,Ab,Bb,Cb,D
Bb,Cb,Db,Eb,Fb,G
Eb,Fb,Gb,Ab,Bbb,C
Ab,Bbb,Cb,Db,Ebb,F
Db,Ebb,Fb,Gb,Abb,Bb
Gb,ABb,Bbb,Cb,Dbb,Eb

Lydian ^2 RagA,Kuksumakaram
C,^D,E,^F,G,A,B
G,^A,B,^C,D,E,^F
D,^E,^F,^G,A,B,^C
A,^B,^C,^D,E,^F,^G
E,^F^ ^G,^A,B,^C,^D
B,^C^ ^D,^E,^F,^G,^A
^F,^G^ ^A,^B,^C,^D,^E
F,^G,A,B,C,D,E
Bb,^C,D,E,F,G,A
Eb,^F,G,A,Bb,C,D
Ab,B,C,D,Eb,F,G
Db,E,F,G,Ab,Bb,C
Gb,A,Bb,C,Db,Eb,F

Locrian Natural Maj 6, Pseudo Turkish
C,Db,Eb,F,Gb,A,Bb
G,Ab,Bb,C,Db,E,F
D,Eb,F,G,Ab,B,C
A,Bb,C,D,Eb,^F,G
E,F,G,A,Bb,^C,D
B,C,D,E,F,^G,A
^F,G,A,B,C,^D,E
F,Gb,Ab,Bb,Cb,D,Eb
Bb,Cb,Db,Eb,Fb,G,Ab
Eb,Fb,Gb,Ab,Bbb,C,Db
Ab,Bbb,Cb,Db,Ebb,F,Gb
Db,Ebb,Fb,Gb,Abb,Bb,Cb
Gb,Abb,Bbb,Cb,Dbb,Eb,Fb

Indian, Phrygian dim 4th
C,Db,Eb,E,G,Ab,Bb
G,Ab,Bb,B,D,Eb,F
D,Eb,F,^F,A,Bb,C
A,Bb,C,^C,E,F,G
E,F,G,^G,B,C,D
B,C,D,^D,^F,G,A
^F,G,A,^A,^C,D,E
F,Gb,Ab,A,C,Db,Eb
Bb,Cb,Db,D,F,Gb,Ab
Eb,Fb,Gb,G,Bb,Cb,Db
Ab,Bbb,Cb,C,Eb,Fb,Gb
Db,Ebb,Fb,F,Ab,Bbb,Cb
Gb,Abb,Bbb,Bb,Db,Ebb,Fb

ChromatiC,Hypodorian
C,D,^D,E,G,^G,A
G,A,^A,B,D,^D,E
D,E,^E,^F,A,^A,B
A,B,^B,^C,E,^E,^F
E,^F,^F^ ^G,B,^B,^C
B,^C,^C^ ^D,^F,^F^ ^G
^F,^G,^G^ ^A,^C,^C^ ^D
F,G,^G,A,C,^C,D
Bb,C,^C,D,F,^F,G
Eb,F,^F,G,Bb,B,C
Ab,Bb,B,C,Eb,E,F
Db,Eb,E,F,Ab,A,Bb
Gb,Ab,A,Bb,Db,D,Eb

ChromatiC,Dorian
C,^C,D,F,G,^G,A
G,^G,A,C,D,^D,E
D,^D,E,G,A,^A,B
A,^A,B,D,E,^E,^F
E,^E,^F,A,B,^B,^C
B,^B,^C,E,^F,^F^ ^G
^F,^F^ ^G,B,^C,^C^ ^D
F,^F,G,Bb,C,^C,D
Bb,B,C,Eb,F,^F,G
Eb,E,F,Ab,Bb,B,C
Ab,A,Bb,Db,Eb,E,F
Db,D,Eb,Gb,Ab,A,Bb
Gb,G,Ab,Cb,Db,D,Eb

ChromatiC,Mixolydian
C,^C,D,F,^F,G,Bb
G,^G,A,C,^C,D,F
D,^D,E,G,^G,A,C
A,^A,B,D,^D,E,G
E,^E,^F,A,^A,B,D
B,^B,^C,E,^E,^F,A
^F,^F^ ^G,B,^B,^C,E
F,^F,G,Bb,B,C,Eb
Bb,B,C,Eb,E,F,Ab
Eb,E,F,Ab,A,Bb,Db
Ab,A,Bb,Db,D,Eb,Gb
Db,D,Eb,Gb,G,Ab,Cb
Gb,G,Ab,Cb,C,Db,Fb

Super Locrian all sharps
C,^C,^D,E,^F,^G,^A
G,^G,^A,B,^C,^D,^E
D,^D,^E,^F,^G,^A,^B
A,^A,^B,^C,^D,^E,^F^
E,^E,^F^ ^G,^A,^B,^C^
B,^B,^C^ ^D,^E,^F^ ^G^
^F,^F^ ^G^ ^A,^B,^C^ ^D^
F,^F,^G,A,B,^C,^D
Bb,B,^C,D,E,^F,^G
Eb,E,^F,G,A,B,^C
Ab,A,B,C,D,E,^F
Db,D,E,F,G,A,B
Gb,G,A,Bb,C,D,E

Prometheus (samE,as 82483 in 12edo)
C,D,E,Gb,A,Bb
G,A,B,Db,E,F
D,E,^F,Ab,B,C
A,B,^C,Eb,^F,G
E,^F,^G,Bb,^C,D
B,^C,^D,F,^G,A
^F,^G,^A,C,^D,E
F,G,A,Cb,D,Eb
Bb,C,D,Fb,G,Ab
Eb,F,G,Bbb,C,Db
Ab,Bb,C,Ebb,F,Gb
Db,Eb,F,Abb,Bb,Cb
Gb,Ab,Bb,Dbb,Eb,Fb

Mixolydian b5
C,D,E,F,Gb,A,Bb
G,A,B,C,Db,E,F
D,E,^F,G,Ab,B,C
A,B,^C,D,Eb,^F,G
E,^F,^G,A,Bb,^C,D
B,^C,^D,E,F,^G,A
^F,^G,^A,B,C,^D,E
F,G,A,Bb,Cb,D,Eb
Bb,C,D,Eb,Fb,G,Ab
Eb,F,G,Ab,Bbb,C,Db
Ab,Bb,C,Db,Ebb,F,Gb
Db,Eb,F,Gb,Abb,Bb,Cb
Gb,Ab,Bb,Cb,Dbb,Eb,Fb

Lydian Minor, Stravinski RagA,RatipriyA,(India)
C,D,E,^F,G,Ab,Bb
G,A,B,^C,D,Eb,F
D,E,^F,^G,A,Bb,C
A,B,^C,^D,E,F,G
E,^F,^G,^A,B,C,D
B,^C,^D,^E,^F,G,A
^F,^G,^A,^B,^C,D,E
F,G,A,B,C,Db,Eb
Bb,C,D,E,F,Gb,Ab
Eb,F,G,A,Bb,Cb,Db
Ab,Bb,C,D,Eb,Fb,Gb
Db,Eb,F,G,Ab,Bbb,Cb
Gb,Ab,Bb,C,Db,Ebb,Fb

Major Locrian
C,D,E,F,Gb,Ab,Bb
G,A,B,C,Db,Eb,F
D,E,^F,G,Ab,Bb,C
A,B,^C,D,Eb,F,G
E,^F,^G,A,Bb,C,D
B,^C,^D,E,F,G,A
^F,^G,^A,B,C,D,E
F,G,A,Bb,Cb,Db,Eb
Bb,C,D,Eb,Fb,Gb,Ab
Eb,F,G,Ab,Bbb,Cb,Db
Ab,Bb,C,Db,Ebb,Fb,Gb
Db,Eb,F,Gb,Abb,Bbb,Cb
Gb,Ab,Bb,Cb,Dbb,Ebb,Fb

Mixolydian Augmented
C,D,E,F,^G,A,Bb
G,A,B,C,^D,E,F
D,E,^F,G,^A,B,C
A,B,^C,D,^E,^F,G
E,^F,^G,A,^B,^C,D
B,^C,^D,E,^F^ ^G,A
^F,^G,^A,B,^C^ ^D,E
F,G,A,Bb,^C,D,Eb
Bb,C,D,Eb,^F,G,Ab
Eb,F,G,Ab,B,C,Db
Ab,Bb,C,Db,E,F,Gb
Db,Eb,F,Gb,A,Bb,Cb
Gb,Ab,Bb,Cb,D,Eb,Fb

ChromatiC,Mixolydian Inverse
C,D,F,^F,G,^A,B
G,A,C,^C,D,^E,^F
D,E,G,^G,A,^B,^C
A,B,D,^D,E,^F^ ^G
E,^F,A,^A,B,^C^ ^D
B,^C,E,^E,^F,^G^ ^A
^F,^G,B,^B,^C,^D^ ^E
F,G,Bb,B,C,^D,E
Bb,C,Eb,E,F,^G,A
Eb,F,Ab,A,Bb,^C,D
Ab,Bb,Db,D,Eb,^F,G
Db,Eb,Gb,G,Ab,B,C
Gb,Ab,Cb,C,Db,E,F

Aeolian Flat 1?
C,Eb,E,Gb,Ab,A,B
G,Bb,B,Db,Eb,E,^F
D,F,^F,Ab,Bb,B,^C
A,C,^C,Eb,F,^F,^G
E,G,^G,Bb,C,^C,^D
B,D,^D,F,G,^G,^A
^F,A,^A,C,D,^D,^E
F,Ab,A,Cb,Db,D,E
Bb,Db,D,Fb,Gb,G,A
Eb,Gb,G,Bbb,Cb,C,D
Ab,Cb,C,Ebb,Fb,F,G
Db,Fb,F,Abb,Bbb,Bb,C
Gb,Bbb,Bb,Dbb,Ebb,Eb,F

Locrian 2
C,D,Eb,F,Gb,Ab,B
G,A,Bb,C,Db,Eb,^F
D,E,F,G,Ab,Bb,^C
A,B,C,D,Eb,F,^G
E,^F,G,A,Bb,C,^D
B,^C,D,E,F,G,^A
^F,^G,A,B,C,D,^E
F,G,Ab,Bb,Cb,Db,E
Bb,C,Db,Eb,Fb,Gb,A
Eb,F,Gb,Ab,Bbb,Cb,D
Ab,Bb,Cb,Db,Ebb,Fb,G
Db,Eb,Fb,Gb,Abb,Bbb,C
Gb,Ab,Bbb,Cb,Dbb,Ebb,F

Blues Phrygian (samE,as 737 in 12 edo)
C,Db,Eb,F,^F,G,Bb
G,Ab,Bb,C,^C,D,F
D,Eb,F,G,^G,A,C
A,Bb,C,D,^D,E,G
E,F,G,A,^A,B,D
B,C,D,E,^E,^F,A
^F,G,A,B,^B,^C,E
F,Gb,Ab,Bb,B,C,Eb
Bb,Cb,Db,Eb,E,F,Ab
Eb,Fb,Gb,Ab,A,Bb,Db
Ab,Bbb,Cb,Db,D,Eb,Gb
Db,Ebb,Fb,Gb,G,Ab,Cb
Gb,Abb,Bbb,Cb,C,Db,Fb

ChromatiC,Phrygian
C,^D,E,F,^G,^A,B
G,^A,B,C,^D,^E,^F
D,^E,^F,G,^A,^B,^C
A,^B,^C,D,^E,^F^ ^G
E,^F^ ^G,A,^B,^C^ ^D
B,^C^ ^D,E,^F^ ^G^ ^A
^F,^G^ ^A,B,^C^ ^D^ ^E
F,^G,A,Bb,^C,^D,E
Bb,^C,D,Eb,^F,^G,A
Eb,^F,G,Ab,B,^C,D
Ab,B,C,Db,E,^F,G
Db,E,F,Gb,A,B,C
Gb,A,Bb,Cb,D,E,F

ChromatiC,Hypolydian, Puravi bVI
C,Db,E,^F,G,Ab,B
G,Ab,B,^C,D,Eb,^F
D,Eb,^F,^G,A,Bb,^C
A,Bb,^C,^D,E,F,^G
E,F,^G,^A,B,C,^D
B,C,^D,^E,^F,G,^A
^F,G,^A,^B,^C,D,^E
F,Gb,A,B,C,Db,E
Bb,Cb,D,E,F,Gb,A
Eb,Fb,G,A,Bb,Cb,D
Ab,Bbb,C,D,Eb,Fb,G
Db,Ebb,F,G,Ab,Bbb,C
Gb,Abb,Bb,C,Db,Ebb,F

ChromatiC,Lydian
C,Db,E,F,Gb,A,B
G,Ab,B,C,Db,E,^F
D,Eb,^F,G,Ab,B,^C
A,Bb,^C,D,Eb,^F,^G
E,F,^G,A,Bb,^C,^D
B,C,^D,E,F,^G,^A
^F,G,^A,B,C,^D,^E
F,Gb,A,Bb,Cb,D,E
Bb,Cb,D,Eb,Fb,G,A
Eb,Fb,G,Ab,Bbb,C,D
Ab,Bbb,C,Db,Ebb,F,G
Db,Ebb,F,Gb,Abb,Bb,C
Gb,Abb,Bb,Cb,Dbb,Eb,F

Aeolian Flat 1

C,Eb,E,Gb,Ab,A,Cb
G,Bb,B,Db,Eb,E,Gb
D,F,^F,Ab,Bb,B,Db
A,C,^C,Eb,F,^F,Ab
E,G,^G,Bb,C,^C,Eb
B,D,^D,F,G,^G,Bb
^F,A,^A,C,D,^D,F
F,Ab,A,Cb,Db,D,Fb
Bb,Db,D,Fb,Gb,G,Bbb
Eb,Gb,G,Bbb,Cb,C,Ebb
Ab,Cb,C,Ebb,Fb,F,Abb
Db,Fb,F,Abb,Bbb,Bb,Dbb
Gb,Bbb,Bb,Dbb,Ebb,Eb,Gbb

Mixolydian Pentatonic ?

C,E,F,G,^A
G,B,C,D,^E
D,^F,G,A,^B
A,^C,D,E,^F^
E,^G,A,B,^C^
B,^D,E,^F,^G^
^F,^A,B,^C,^D^
F,A,Bb,C,^D
Bb,D,Eb,F,^G
Eb,G,Ab,Bb,^C
Ab,C,Db,Eb,^F
Db,F,Gb,Ab,B
Gb,Bb,Cb,Db,E

Moorish Phrygian 4 ^-s
C,^C,^D,E,F,G,^G,^A,B
G,^G,^A,B,C,D,^D,^E,^F
D,^D,^E,^F,G,A,^A,^B,^C
A,^A,^B,^C,D,E,^E,^F^ ^G
E,^E,^F^ ^G,A,B,^B,^C^ ^D
B,^B,^C^ ^D,E,^F,^F^ ^G^ ^A
^F,^F^ ^G^ ^A,B,^C,^C^ ^D^ ^E
F,^F,^G,A,Bb,C,^C,^D,E
Bb,B,^C,D,Eb,F,^F,^G,A
Eb,E,^F,G,Ab,Bb,B,^C,D
Ab,A,B,C,Db,Eb,E,^F,G
Db,D,E,F,Gb,Ab,A,B,C
Gb,G,A,Bb,Cb,Db,D,E,F

ChromatiC,Dorian InversE,RagA,NonE,(India)
C,^D,E,F,G,^A,B
G,^A,B,C,D,^E,^F
D,^E,^F,G,A,^B,^C
A,^B,^C,D,E,^F^ ^G
E,^F^ ^G,A,B,^C^ ^D
B,^C^ ^D,E,^F,^G^ ^A
^F,^G^ ^A,B,^C,^D^ ^E
F,^G,A,Bb,C,^D,E
Bb,^C,D,Eb,F,^G,A
Eb,^F,G,Ab,Bb,^C,D
Ab,B,C,Db,Eb,^F,G
Db,E,F,Gb,Ab,B,C
Gb,A,Bb,Cb,Db,E,F

ChromatiC,Hypodorian Inverse
C,^D,E,F,^G,A,Bb
G,^A,B,C,^D,E,F
D,^E,^F,G,^A,B,C
A,^B,^C,D,^E,^F,G
E,^F^ ^G,A,^B,^C,D
B,^C^ ^D,E,^F^ ^G,A
^F,^G^ ^A,B,^C^ ^D,E
F,^G,A,Bb,^C,D,Eb
Bb,^C,D,Eb,^F,G,Ab
Eb,^F,G,Ab,B,C,Db
Ab,B,C,Db,E,F,Gb
Db,E,F,Gb,A,Bb,Cb
Gb,A,Bb,Cb,D,Eb,Fb

ChromatiC,Lydian Inverse, Todi bVI
C,Db,Eb,^F,G,Ab,B
G,Ab,Bb,^C,D,Eb,^F
D,Eb,F,^G,A,Bb,^C
A,Bb,C,^D,E,F,^G
E,F,G,^A,B,C,^D
B,C,D,^E,^F,G,^A
^F,G,A,^B,^C,D,^E
F,Gb,Ab,B,C,Db,E
Bb,Cb,Db,E,F,Gb,A
Eb,Fb,Gb,A,Bb,Cb,D
Ab,Bbb,Cb,D,Eb,Fb,G
Db,Ebb,Fb,G,Ab,Bbb,C
Gb,Abb,Bbb,C,Db,Ebb,F

ChromatiC,Hypolydian Inverse, Persian
C,Db,E,F,Gb,Ab,B
G,Ab,B,C,Db,Eb,^F
D,Eb,^F,G,Ab,Bb,^C
A,Bb,^C,D,Eb,F,^G
E,F,^G,A,Bb,C,^D
B,C,^D,E,F,G,^A
^F,G,^A,B,C,D,^E
F,Gb,A,Bb,Cb,Db,E
Bb,Cb,D,Eb,Fb,Gb,A
Eb,Fb,G,Ab,Bbb,Cb,D
Ab,Bbb,C,Db,Ebb,Fb,G
Db,Ebb,F,Gb,Abb,Bbb,C
Gb,Abb,Bb,Cb,Dbb,Ebb,F

ChromatiC,Mixolydian
C,^C,D,F,^F,G,^A
G,^G,A,C,^C,D,^E
D,^D,E,G,^G,A,^B
A,^A,B,D,^D,E,^F^
E,^E,^F,A,^A,B,^C^
B,^B,^C,E,^E,^F,^G^
^F,^F^ ^G,B,^B,^C,^D^
F,^F,G,Bb,B,C,^D
Bb,B,C,Eb,E,F,^G
Eb,E,F,Ab,A,Bb,^C
Ab,A,Bb,Db,D,Eb,^F
Db,D,Eb,Gb,G,Ab,B
Gb,G,Ab,Cb,C,Db,E

Moorish Phrygian 2b2^ expected
C,^C,Eb,E,F,G,^G,Bb,B
G,^G,Bb,B,C,D,^D,F,^F
D,^D,F,^F,G,A,^A,C,^C
A,^A,C,^C,D,E,^E,G,^G
E,^E,G,^G,A,B,^B,D,^D
B,^B,D,^D,E,^F,^F^ A,^A
^F,^F^ A,^A,B,^C,^C^ E,^E
F,^F,Ab,A,Bb,C,^C,Eb,E
Bb,B,Db,D,Eb,F,^F,Ab,A
Eb,E,Gb,G,Ab,Bb,B,Db,D
Ab,A,Cb,C,Db,Eb,E,Gb,G
Db,D,Fb,F,Gb,Ab,A,Cb,C
Gb,G,Bbb,Bb,Cb,Db,D,Fb,F

Moorish Phrygian 3b1^ expected
C,^C,Eb,E,F,G,Ab,Bb,B
G,^G,Bb,B,C,D,Eb,F,^F
D,^D,F,^F,G,A,Bb,C,^C
A,^A,C,^C,D,E,F,G,^G
E,^E,G,^G,A,B,C,D,^D
B,^B,D,^D,E,^F,G,A,^A
^F,^F^ A,^A,B,^C,D,E,^E
F,^F,Ab,A,Bb,C,Db,Eb,E
Bb,B,Db,D,Eb,F,Gb,Ab,A
Eb,E,Gb,G,Ab,Bb,Cb,Db,D
Ab,A,Cb,C,Db,Eb,Fb,Gb,G
Db,D,Fb,F,Gb,Ab,Bbb,Cb,C
Gb,G,Bbb,Bb,Cb,Db,Ebb,Fb,F

ChromatiC,DiatoniC,Dorian (^1,b3,^5,b7)
C,^C,D,Eb,F,G,^G,A,Bb
G,^G,A,Bb,C,D,^D,E,F
D,^D,E,F,G,A,^A,B,C
A,^A,B,C,D,E,^E,^F,G
E,^E,^F,G,A,B,^B,^C,D
B,^B,^C,D,E,^F,^F^ ^G,A
^F,^F^ ^G,A,B,^C,^C^ ^D,E
F,^F,G,Ab,Bb,C,^C,D,Eb
Bb,B,C,Db,Eb,F,^F,G,Ab
Eb,E,F,Gb,Ab,Bb,B,C,Db
Ab,A,Bb,Cb,Db,Eb,E,F,Gb
Db,D,Eb,Fb,Gb,Ab,A,Bb,Cb
Gb,G,Ab,Bbb,Cb,Db,D,Eb,Fb

Dorian Aeolian (as 705 in 12 edo)
C,D,Eb,F,G,^G,A,Bb
G,A,Bb,C,D,^D,E,F
D,E,F,G,A,^A,B,C
A,B,C,D,E,^E,^F,G
E,^F,G,A,B,^B,^C,D
B,^C,D,E,^F,^F^ ^G,A
^F,^G,A,B,^C,^C^ ^D,E
F,G,Ab,Bb,C,^C,D,Eb
Bb,C,Db,Eb,F,^F,G,Ab
Eb,F,Gb,Ab,Bb,B,C,Db
Ab,Bb,Cb,Db,Eb,E,F,Gb
Db,Eb,Fb,Gb,Ab,A,Bb,Cb
Gb,Ab,Bbb,Cb,Db,D,Eb,Fb

Phrygian Aeolian 3b1^
C,^C,D,Eb,F,G,Ab,Bb
G,^G,A,Bb,C,D,Eb,F
D,^D,E,F,G,A,Bb,C
A,^A,B,C,D,E,F,G
E,^E,^F,G,A,B,C,D
B,^B,^C,D,E,^F,G,A
^F,^F^ ^G,A,B,^C,D,E
F,^F,G,Ab,Bb,C,Db,Eb
Bb,B,C,Db,Eb,F,Gb,Ab
Eb,E,F,Gb,Ab,Bb,Cb,Db
Ab,A,Bb,Cb,Db,Eb,Fb,Gb
Db,D,Eb,Fb,Gb,Ab,Bbb,Cb
Gb,G,Ab,Bbb,Cb,Db,Ebb,Fb

Phrygian Locrian (samE,as 707 in 12 edo)
C,Db,Eb,F,^F,G,Ab,Bb
G,Ab,Bb,C,^C,D,Eb,F
D,Eb,F,G,^G,A,Bb,C
A,Bb,C,D,^D,E,F,G
E,F,G,A,^A,B,C,D
B,C,D,E,^E,^F,G,A
^F,G,A,B,^B,^C,D,E
F,Gb,Ab,Bb,B,C,Db,Eb
Bb,Cb,Db,Eb,E,F,Gb,Ab
Eb,Fb,Gb,Ab,A,Bb,Cb,Db
Ab,Bbb,Cb,Db,D,Eb,Fb,Gb
Db,Ebb,Fb,Gb,G,Ab,Bbb,Cb
Gb,Abb,Bbb,Cb,C,Db,Ebb,Fb

Lydian Mixolydian Taishikicho, Ryo (Japan)
C,D,E,F,^F,G,A,^A,B
G,A,B,C,^C,D,E,^E,^F
D,E,^F,G,^G,A,B,^B,^C
A,B,^C,D,^D,E,^F,^F^ ^G
E,^F,^G,A,^A,B,^C,^C^ ^D
B,^C,^D,E,^E,^F,^G,^G^ ^A
^F,^G,^A,B,^B,^C,^D,^D^ ^E
F,G,A,Bb,B,C,D,^D,E
Bb,C,D,Eb,E,F,G,^G,A
Eb,F,G,Ab,A,Bb,C,^C,D
Ab,Bb,C,Db,D,Eb,F,^F,G
Db,Eb,F,Gb,G,Ab,Bb,B,C
Gb,Ab,Bb,Cb,C,Db,Eb,E,F

UltrA,Locrian
C,Db,^D,E,^F,^G,A
G,Ab,^A,B,^C,^D,E
D,Eb,^E,^F,^G,^A,B
A,Bb,^B,^C,^D,^E,^F
E,F,^F^ ^G,^A,^B,^C
B,C,^C^ ^D,^E,^F^ ^G
^F,G,^G^ ^A,^B,^C^ ^D
F,Gb,^G,A,B,^C,D
Bb,Cb,^C,D,E,^F,G
Eb,Fb,^F,G,A,B,C
Ab,Bbb,B,C,D,E,F
Db,Ebb,E,F,G,A,Bb
Gb,Abb,A,Bb,C,D,Eb

Blues Dorian Hexatonic
C,Db,^D,E,G,A
G,Ab,^A,B,D,E
D,Eb,^E,^F,A,B
A,Bb,^B,^C,E,^F
E,F,^F^ ^G,B,^C
B,C,^C^ ^D,^F,^G
^F,G,^G^ ^A,^C,^D
F,Gb,^G,A,C,D
Bb,Cb,^C,D,F,G
Eb,Fb,^F,G,Bb,C
Ab,Bbb,B,C,Eb,F
Db,Ebb,E,F,Ab,Bb
Gb,Abb,A,Bb,Db,Eb

Indian, Phrygian dim 4th
C,Db,^D,E,G,Ab,Bb
G,Ab,^A,B,D,Eb,F
D,Eb,^E,^F,A,Bb,C
A,Bb,^B,^C,E,F,G
E,F,^F^ ^G,B,C,D
B,C,^C^ ^D,^F,G,A
^F,G,^G^ ^A,^C,D,E
F,Gb,^G,A,C,Db,Eb
Bb,Cb,^C,D,F,Gb,Ab
Eb,Fb,^F,G,Bb,Cb,Db
Ab,Bbb,B,C,Eb,Fb,Gb
Db,Ebb,E,F,Ab,Bbb,Cb
Gb,Abb,A,Bb,Db,Ebb,Fb

Phrygian Major, Flamenco, Spanish Phrygian
C,Db,^D,E,F,G,Ab,Bb
G,Ab,^A,B,C,D,Eb,F
D,Eb,^E,^F,G,A,Bb,C
A,Bb,^B,^C,D,E,F,G
E,F,^F^ ^G,A,B,C,D
B,C,^C^ ^D,E,^F,G,A
^F,G,^G^ ^A,B,^C,D,E
F,Gb,^G,A,Bb,C,Db,Eb
Bb,Cb,^C,D,Eb,F,Gb,Ab
Eb,Fb,^F,G,Ab,Bb,Cb,Db
Ab,Bbb,B,C,Db,Eb,Fb,Gb
Db,Ebb,E,F,Gb,Ab,Bbb,Cb
Gb,Abb,A,Bb,Cb,Db,Ebb,Fb

Moorish Phrygian 2b2^ spread
C,Db,^D,E,F,G,Ab,^A,B
G,Ab,^A,B,C,D,Eb,^E,^F
D,Eb,^E,^F,G,A,Bb,^B,^C
A,Bb,^B,^C,D,E,F,^F^ ^G
E,F,^F^ ^G,A,B,C,^C^ ^D
B,C,^C^ ^D,E,^F,G,^G^ ^A
^F,G,^G^ ^A,B,^C,D,^D^ ^E
F,Gb,^G,A,Bb,C,Db,^D,E
Bb,Cb,^C,D,Eb,F,Gb,^G,A
Eb,Fb,^F,G,Ab,Bb,Cb,^C,D
Ab,Bbb,B,C,Db,Eb,Fb,^F,G
Db,Ebb,E,F,Gb,Ab,Bbb,B,C
Gb,Abb,A,Bb,Cb,Db,Ebb,E,F

Superlocrian, DiminisheD,Whole-TonE,(as 8289 in 12 edo)
C,Db,^D,E,Gb,Ab,Bb
G,Ab,^A,B,Db,Eb,F
D,Eb,^E,^F,Ab,Bb,C
A,Bb,^B,^C,Eb,F,G
E,F,^F^ ^G,Bb,C,D
B,C,^C^ ^D,F,G,A
^F,G,^G^ ^A,C,D,E
F,Gb,^G,A,Cb,Db,Eb
Bb,Cb,^C,D,Fb,Gb,Ab
Eb,Fb,^F,G,Bbb,Cb,Db
Ab,Bbb,B,C,Ebb,Fb,Gb
Db,Ebb,E,F,Abb,Bbb,Cb
Gb,Abb,A,Bb,Dbb,Ebb,Fb

Mode or Scale	Celestial Sphere	Day of Week	Muse	Element	Humor	Musical Note (Major Scale)
8. Hypomixolydian	Fixed Stars		Urania	Earth	Melancholic	---
7. Mixolydian	Saturn	Saturday	Polyhymnia	Earth	Melancholic	D
6. Lydian	Jupiter	Thursday	Euterpe	Air	Sanguine	C
5. Phrygian	Mars	Tuesday	Erato	Fire	Choleric	B
4. Dorian	Sun	Sunday	Melpomene	Water	Phlegmatic	A
3. Hypolydian	Venus	Friday	Terpsichore	Air	Sanguine	G
2. Hypophrygian	Mercury	Wednesday	Calliope	Fire	Choleric	F
1. Hypodorian	Moon	Monday	Clio	Water	Phlegmatic	E
---	Earth		Thalia			Silence

C Lydian	C	D	E	F#	G	A	B	C
F Lydian	F	G	A	B	C	D	E	F
Bb Lydian	Bb	C	D	E	F	G	A	Bb
Eb Lydian	Eb	F	G	A	Bb	C	D	Eb
Ab Lydian	Ab	Bb	C	D	Eb	F	G	Ab
Db Lydian	Db	Eb	F	G	Ab	Bb	C	Db
Gb Lydian	Gb	Ab	Bb	C	Db	Eb	F	Gb
B Lydian	B	C#	D#	E# (F)	F#	G#	A#	B
E Lydian	E	F#	G#	A# (Bb)	B	C#	D#	E
A Lydian	A	B	C#	D#	E	F#	G#	A
D Lydian	D	E	F#	G#	A	B	C#	D
G Lydian	G	A	B	C#	D	E	F#	G

Medieval church modes
mode I Dorian D,E,F,G,A,B,C,D,E
mode II Hypodorian A,B,C,D,E,F,G,A,B
mode III Phrygian E,F,G,A,B,C,D,E,F
mode IV Hypophrygian B,C,D,E,F,G,A,B,C
mode V Lydian F,G,A,B,C,D,E,F,G
mode VI Hypolydian C,D,E,F,G,A,B,C,D
mode VII Mixolydian G,A,B,C,D,E,F,G,A
mode VIII Hypomixolydian D,E,F,G,A,B,C,D,E

16th century eight-mode system of the Gregorian
mode IX Aeolian A,B,C,D,E,F,G,A,B
mode X Hypoaeolian E,F,G,A,B,C,D,E,F
mode XI Ionian C,D,E,F,G,A,B,C,D
mode XII Hypoionian G,A,B,C,D,E,F,G,A

Medieval and middle ages
mode XIII Locrian B,C,D,E,F,G,A,B,C
mode XIV Hypolocrian F,G,A,B,C,D,E,F,G

Authentic modes
Ionian (major) C,D,E,F,G,A,B,C,D
Dorian D,E,F,G,A,B,C,D,E
Phrygian E,F,G,A,B,C,D,E,F
Lydian F,G,A,B,C,D,E,F,G
Mixolydian G,A,B,C,D,E,F,G,A
Aeolian (minor) A,B,C,D,E,F,G,A,B
Locrian B,D,C,E,F,G,A,B,D

Saturn (Hypodorian Mode)
^F,G,^A,B,C,D,E,^F

Jupiter (Hypophrygian Mode)
E,^F,G,^A,B,C,D,E

Mars (Hypolydian Mode)
D,E,^F,^G,^A,B,C,D

Sun (Dorian Mode)
C,D,E,^F,^G,^A,B,C

Venus-1 (Phrygian Mode)
B,C,D,E,^F,G,^A,B

Venus-2 (Phrygian Mode)
B,C,D,E,^F,^G,^A,B

Mercury (Lydian Scale)
^A,B,C,D,E,^F,G,^A

Moon (Mixolydian Scale)
^G,^A,B,C,D,E,^F,^G

Dorian Mode Species (Mars)
C,D,E,^F,^G,^A,B,C

Hypolydian Species (Mars)
D,E,^F,G,^A,B,C,D

Hypophrygian Species (Jupiter)
E,^F,G,^A,B,C,D,E

Hypodorian Species (Saturn)
^F,G,^A,B,C,D,E,^F

Mixolydian Species (Moon)
^G,^A,B,C,D,E,^F,^G

Ptolemaic 18 keys

Gb major 7 flats
Cb,Db,Eb,Fb,Gb,Ab,Bb,Cb,Db

Gb major 6 flats
Gb,Ab,Bb,Cb,Db,Eb,F,G,A

Db major 5 flats
Db,Eb,F,Gb,Ab,Bb,C,Db,Eb

Ab major 4 flats
Ab,Bb,C,Db,Eb,F,G,Ab,Bb

Eb major 3 flats
Eb,F,G,Ab,Bb,C,D,Eb,F

Bb major 2 flats
Bb,C,D,Eb,F,G,A,Bb,C

F major 1 flat
F,G,A,Bb,C,D,E,F,G

C major 0 flat
C,D,E,F,G,A,B,C,D

G major 1 sharp
G,A,B,C,D,E,^F,G,A

D major 2 sharps
D,E,^F,G,A,B,^C,D,E

A major 3 sharps
A,B,^C,D,E,^F,^G,A,B

E major 4 sharps
E,^F,^G,A,B,^C,^D,E,^F

B major 5 sharps
B,^C,^D,E,^F,^G,^A,B,^C

^F major 6 sharps
^F,^G,^A,B,^C,^D,^E,^F,^G

^C major 7 sharps
^C,^D,^E,^F,^G,^A,^B,^C,^D

Major Third
C,D,E,F,G,A,B,C,D

Ptolemaic Tuning-1
F,A,C,E,G,B,D,F,A

Ptolemaic Tuning-2
C,D,E,F,G,A,B,C,D

new 19 different keys

Enharmonic Ptolemaic
^C,^D,E,^E,^F,^G,^A,B,^B

Enharmonic Ptolemaic
Db,Eb,Fb,F,Gb,Ab,Bb,Cb,C

Shaded inside circle
C,G,D,A,E,B,^F,C,G

Unshaded outside circle
E,B,^F,^C,^G,^D,^A,Eb,Bb

Interleaved circle
C,E,G,B,D,^F,A,C,E

Ptolemaic fifths
C,D,E,F,G,A,B,C,D

Ptolemaic chords
F,A,C,E,G,B,D,F,A

Temperament System

C,D,E,F,G,A,B,C',D'

C,D,Eb,F,G,Ab,B,C',D'

C,D,E,F,G,A,Bb,C',D'

C,D,E,F,G,Ab,Bb,C',D'

C,D,Eb,F,G,A,B,C',D'

C,D,Eb,F,G,A,Bb,C',D'

C,D,Eb,F,G,Ab,Bb,C',D'

C,Db,Eb,F,G,A,B,C',D'

C,Db,Eb,F,G,A,Bb,C',D'

C,Db,Eb,F,G,Ab,Bb,C',D'

C,D,E,^F,G,A,B,C',D'

C,Db,Eb,F,Gb,Ab,Bb,C',D'

Greek 18 notes System

'υπάτη υπάτων' 'λιχανός υπάτων διάτονος' 'παρυπάτη υπάτων' 'παρυπάτη υπάτων' 'παρυπάτη υπάτων' 'υπάτη μέσων'

To Vulcan

'τρίτη συνημμένων' 'λιχανός μέσων διάτονος' 'μέση' 'τρίτη συνημμένων' 'παρυπάτη υπάτων' 'μέση' 'λιχανός μέσων διάτονος' 'λιχανός υπάτων διάτονος' 'υπάτη μέσων'

Orphic Hymn

'λιχανός υπάτων διάτονος' 'παρυπάτη υπάτων' 'τρίτη συνημμένων' 'παρυπάτη υπάτων' 'υπάτη υπάτων' 'λιχανός μέσων διάτονος' 'λιχανός μέσων διάτονος' 'τρίτη συνημμένων' 'υπάτη μέσων' 'λιχανός μέσων διάτονος' 'τρίτη συνημμένων' 'λιχανός μέσων διάτονος' 'μέση' 'τρίτη συνημμένων' 'μέση'

Music by Gregory Zorzos

'υπάτη υπάτων' 'τρίτη συνημμένων' 'υπάτη μέσων' 'λιχανός μέσων διάτονος'

STRONG,
'λιχανός υπάτων διάτονος' 'τρίτη συνημμένων' 'λιχανός μέσων διάτονος' 'μέση' 'υπάτη υπάτων' 'λιχανός μέσων διάτονος' 'λιχανός υπάτων διάτονος' 'παρυπάτη υπάτων' 'παρυπάτη υπάτων' 'παρυπάτη υπάτων' 'υπάτη μέσων'
mighty Vulcan,
'υπάτη υπάτων' 'υπάτη μέσων' 'τρίτη συνημμένων' 'τρίτη συνημμένων' 'υπάτη μέσων' 'λιχανός μέσων διάτονος' 'λιχανός μέσων διάτονος' 'παρυπάτη υπάτων' 'υπάτη μέσων' 'υπάτη μέσων' 'λιχανός υπάτων διάτονος' 'τρίτη συνημμένων' 'λιχανός υπάτων διάτονος' 'παρυπάτη υπάτων' 'τρίτη συνημμένων' 'λιχανός μέσων διάτονος' 'μέση' 'υπάτη υπάτων'
bearing splendid light,
'παρυπάτη υπάτων' 'υπάτη μέσων' 'υπάτη μέσων' 'υπάτη μέσων' 'τρίτη συνημμένων' 'λιχανός μέσων διάτονος' 'λιχανός υπάτων διάτονος' 'τρίτη συνημμένων' 'τρίτη συνημμένων' 'υπάτη μέσων'
Unweary'd fire,
'υπάτη μέσων' 'τρίτη συνημμένων' 'υπάτη υπάτων' 'μέση' 'παρυπάτη υπάτων'

'λιχανός υπάτων διάτονος' 'τρίτη συνημμένων' 'υπάτη μέσων' 'λιχανός μέσων διάτονος' 'υπάτη υπάτων' 'τρίτη συνημμένων' 'τρίτη συνημμένων' 'υπάτη μέσων' 'υπάτη μέσων' 'υπάτη υπάτων' 'υπάτη υπάτων' 'τρίτη συνημμένων' 'τρίτη συνημμένων' 'λιχανός μέσων διάτονος' 'μέση' 'υπάτη υπάτων'
with flaming torrents bright:
'υπάτη υπάτων' 'τρίτη συνημμένων' 'υπάτη μέσων' 'λιχανός μέσων διάτονος' 'μέση' 'υπάτη μέσων' 'λιχανός υπάτων διάτονος' 'υπάτη μέσων' 'λιχανός υπάτων διάτονος'
Strong-handed,
'λιχανός υπάτων διάτονος' 'υπάτη μέσων' 'υπάτη υπάτων' 'μέση' 'παρυπάτη υπάτων' 'υπάτη μέσων'
deathless,
'υπάτη μέσων' 'λιχανός υπάτων διάτονος' 'τρίτη συνημμένων' 'υπάτη υπάτων' 'λιχανός υπάτων διάτονος' 'τρίτη συνημμένων' 'λιχανός υπάτων διάτονος' 'τρίτη συνημμένων' 'υπάτη μέσων' 'υπάτη μέσων'

and of art divine,
'λιχανός μέσων διάτονος' 'παρυπάτη υπάτων' 'τρίτη συνημμένων' 'υπάτη μέσων' 'υπάτη μέσων' 'παρυπάτη υπάτων' 'υπάτη μέσων' 'λιχανός υπάτων διάτονος' 'υπάτη μέσων' 'υπάτη μέσων' 'υπάτη υπάτων'
Pure element,
'λιχανός μέσων διάτονος' 'τρίτη συνημμένων' 'υπάτη υπάτων' 'τρίτη συνημμένων' 'υπάτη μέσων' 'υπάτη υπάτων' 'μέση' 'υπάτη μέσων' 'υπάτη μέσων' 'τρίτη συνημμένων' 'παρυπάτη υπάτων' 'λιχανός υπάτων διάτονος' 'τρίτη συνημμένων' 'υπάτη υπάτων' 'μέση' 'τρίτη συνημμένων' 'υπάτη μέσων' 'υπάτη μέσων'
a portion of the world is thine:
'παρυπάτη υπάτων' 'παρυπάτη υπάτων' 'υπάτη υπάτων' 'λιχανός υπάτων διάτονος' 'τρίτη συνημμένων' 'υπάτη μέσων' 'λιχανός μέσων διάτονος' 'τρίτη συνημμένων' 'υπάτη υπάτων' 'τρίτη συνημμένων' 'υπάτη υπάτων'
All-taming artist,
'παρυπάτη υπάτων' 'παρυπάτη υπάτων' 'λιχανός υπάτων διάτονος' 'τρίτη

συνημμένων' 'παρυπάτη υπάτων' 'τρίτη συνημμένων' 'λιχανός υπάτων διάτονος' 'υπάτη μέσων' 'λιχανός μέσων διάτονος' 'υπάτη μέσων' 'υπάτη μέσων' 'τρίτη συνημμένων'

all-diffusive power,

'υπάτη υπάτων' 'μέση' 'τρίτη συνημμένων' 'υπάτη υπάτων' 'μέση' 'τρίτη συνημμένων' 'υπάτη μέσων' 'υπάτη μέσων' 'παρυπάτη υπάτων' 'λιχανός μέσων διάτονος' 'τρίτη συνημμένων' 'υπάτη μέσων' 'λιχανός υπάτων διάτονος' 'υπάτη μέσων'

'This thine supreme,

'παρυπάτη υπάτων' 'παρυπάτη υπάτων' 'παρυπάτη υπάτων' 'υπάτη υπάτων' 'υπάτη υπάτων' 'υπάτη μέσων' 'παρυπάτη υπάτων' 'υπάτη μέσων' 'υπάτη υπάτων' 'λιχανός υπάτων διάτονος' 'υπάτη μέσων' 'λιχανός υπάτων διάτονος' 'παρυπάτη υπάτων' 'τρίτη συνημμένων'

all substance to devour:

'υπάτη μέσων' 'υπάτη υπάτων' 'μέση' 'υπάτη μέσων' 'τρίτη συνημμένων'

Aether,

'παρυπάτη υπάτων' 'υπάτη μέσων'

Sun,

'λιχανός υπάτων διάτονος' 'υπάτη μέσων'
Moon,
'υπάτη μέσων' 'λιχανός υπάτων διάτονος' 'υπάτη υπάτων' 'τρίτη συνημμένων'
and Stars,
'παρυπάτη υπάτων' 'τρίτη συνημμένων' 'λιχανός μέσων διάτονος' 'μέση' 'υπάτη υπάτων' 'λιχανός μέσων διάτονος' 'παρυπάτη υπάτων' 'τρίτη συνημμένων' 'υπάτη μέσων' 'υπάτη μέσων' 'λιχανός υπάτων διάτονος' 'παρυπάτη υπάτων' 'παρυπάτη υπάτων' 'υπάτη μέσων' 'τρίτη συνημμένων'
light pure and clear,
'τρίτη συνημμένων' 'υπάτη υπάτων' 'μέση' 'υπάτη μέσων' 'υπάτη μέσων' 'υπάτη υπάτων' 'μέση' 'λιχανός μέσων διάτονος' 'παρυπάτη υπάτων' 'παρυπάτη υπάτων' 'παρυπάτη υπάτων' 'τρίτη συνημμένων' 'λιχανός υπάτων διάτονος' 'λιχανός μέσων διάτονος' 'τρίτη συνημμένων' 'υπάτη υπάτων' 'υπάτη υπάτων' 'λιχανός υπάτων διάτονος' 'υπάτη μέσων' 'υπάτη μέσων' 'λιχανός μέσων διάτονος' 'λιχανός μέσων διάτονος' 'υπάτη μέσων' 'τρίτη συνημμένων'

For these thy lucid parts to men appear.
'υπάτη υπάτων' 'υπάτη υπάτων' 'μέση' 'υπάτη μέσων' 'υπάτη μέσων'
To thee,
'παρυπάτη υπάτων' 'παρυπάτη υπάτων' 'λιχανός υπάτων διάτονος' 'υπάτη μέσων' 'υπάτη μέσων' 'παρυπάτη υπάτων' 'παρυπάτη υπάτων' 'τρίτη συνημμένων' 'υπάτη μέσων' 'λιχανός μέσων διάτονος'
all dwellings,
'παρυπάτη υπάτων' 'τρίτη συνημμένων' 'υπάτη υπάτων' 'τρίτη συνημμένων' 'υπάτη μέσων'
cities,
'υπάτη υπάτων' 'τρίτη συνημμένων' 'τρίτη συνημμένων' 'υπάτη υπάτων' 'υπάτη μέσων' 'υπάτη υπάτων' 'υπάτη μέσων' 'παρυπάτη υπάτων' 'υπάτη μέσων' 'λιχανός μέσων διάτονος'
tribes belong,
'λιχανός υπάτων διάτονος' 'τρίτη συνημμένων' 'παρυπάτη υπάτων' 'υπάτη μέσων' 'λιχανός υπάτων διάτονος' 'υπάτη υπάτων' 'μέση' 'τρίτη συνημμένων' 'λιχανός υπάτων διάτονος' 'τρίτη συνημμένων' 'υπάτη υπάτων' 'παρυπάτη

υπάτων' 'υπάτη υπάτων' 'λιχανός υπάτων διάτονος' 'τρίτη συνημμένων' 'υπάτη μέσων' 'υπάτη υπάτων' 'τρίτη συνημμένων' 'τρίτη συνημμένων' 'λιχανός μέσων διάτονος' 'μέση' 'υπάτη υπάτων' 'υπάτη μέσων' 'λιχανός υπάτων διάτονος' 'υπάτη υπάτων' 'τρίτη συνημμένων' 'υπάτη μέσων' 'λιχανός μέσων διάτονος'

Diffused thro' mortal bodies bright and strong.

'μέση' 'υπάτη μέσων' 'τρίτη συνημμένων'

Hear,

'υπάτη υπάτων' 'παρυπάτη υπάτων' 'υπάτη μέσων' 'υπάτη μέσων' 'λιχανός υπάτων διάτονος' 'λιχανός μέσων διάτονος' 'υπάτη μέσων' 'υπάτη μέσων' 'τρίτη συνημμένων'

blessed power,

'υπάτη υπάτων' 'μέση' 'παρυπάτη υπάτων' 'λιχανός μέσων διάτονος' 'τρίτη συνημμένων' 'τρίτη συνημμένων' 'υπάτη υπάτων' 'υπάτη μέσων' 'τρίτη συνημμένων' 'υπάτη μέσων' 'παρυπάτη υπάτων' 'παρυπάτη υπάτων' 'τρίτη συνημμένων' 'υπάτη μέσων' 'υπάτη μέσων'

to holy rites incline,

'υπάτη μέσων' 'λιχανός υπάτων διάτονος' 'παρυπάτη υπάτων' 'παρυπάτη υπάτων' 'λιχανός μέσων διάτονος' 'τρίτη συνημμένων' 'λιχανός μέσων διάτονος' 'τρίτη συνημμένων' 'υπάτη υπάτων' 'τρίτη συνημμένων' 'παρυπάτη υπάτων' 'υπάτη μέσων' 'υπάτη υπάτων' 'μέση' 'υπάτη μέσων' 'τρίτη συνημμένων' 'υπάτη μέσων' 'παρυπάτη υπάτων' 'υπάτη μέσων' 'υπάτη μέσων' 'υπάτη μέσων' 'μέση' 'τρίτη συνημμένων' 'υπάτη μέσων' 'υπάτη μέσων'
And all propitious on the incense shine:
'παρυπάτη υπάτων' 'λιχανός μέσων διάτονος' 'λιχανός μέσων διάτονος' 'τρίτη συνημμένων' 'υπάτη μέσων' 'υπάτη υπάτων' 'μέση' 'υπάτη μέσων' 'τρίτη συνημμένων' 'λιχανός μέσων διάτονος' 'υπάτη μέσων' 'τρίτη συνημμένων' 'τρίτη συνημμένων' 'υπάτη μέσων' 'παρυπάτη υπάτων' 'υπάτη μέσων' 'υπάτη μέσων' 'υπάτη μέσων' 'τρίτη συνημμένων' 'τρίτη συνημμένων' 'υπάτη μέσων' 'λιχανός υπάτων διάτονος' 'τρίτη συνημμένων' 'λιχανός υπάτων διάτονος' 'υπάτη μέσων'

Suspress the rage of fires unwearied frame,
'υπάτη μέσων' 'λιχανός υπάτων διάτονος' 'υπάτη υπάτων' 'τρίτη συνημμένων' 'παρυπάτη υπάτων' 'παρυπάτη υπάτων' 'λιχανός μέσων διάτονος' 'τρίτη συνημμένων' 'υπάτη μέσων' 'υπάτη μέσων' 'τρίτη συνημμένων' 'λιχανός υπάτων διάτονος' 'υπάτη μέσων' 'παρυπάτη υπάτων' 'τρίτη συνημμένων' 'υπάτη μέσων' 'υπάτη υπάτων' 'παρυπάτη υπάτων' 'τρίτη συνημμένων' 'υπάτη μέσων' 'λιχανός υπάτων διάτονος' 'τρίτη συνημμένων' 'υπάτη υπάτων' 'παρυπάτη υπάτων' 'παρυπάτη υπάτων' 'λιχανός υπάτων διάτονος' 'υπάτη μέσων'
And still preserve our nature's vital flame.
'υπάτη υπάτων' 'λιχανός υπάτων διάτονος' 'παρυπάτη υπάτων' 'παρυπάτη υπάτων' 'παρυπάτη υπάτων' 'υπάτη μέσων'
To Vulcan
'τρίτη συνημμένων' 'λιχανός μέσων διάτονος' 'μέση' 'τρίτη συνημμένων' 'παρυπάτη υπάτων' 'μέση' 'λιχανός μέσων διάτονος' 'λιχανός υπάτων διάτονος' 'υπάτη μέσων'

Orphic Hymn

'λιχανός υπάτων διάτονος' 'παρυπάτη υπάτων' 'τρίτη συνημμένων' 'παρυπάτη υπάτων' 'υπάτη υπάτων' 'λιχανός μέσων διάτονος' 'λιχανός μέσων διάτονος' 'τρίτη συνημμένων' 'υπάτη μέσων' 'λιχανός μέσων διάτονος' 'τρίτη συνημμένων' 'λιχανός μέσων διάτονος' 'μέση' 'τρίτη συνημμένων' 'μέση'

Music by Gregory Zorzos

160 DATA **Chakra energy**
Transpersonal,^C,^D,^E,^F,^G,^A,^B,^C,^D
170 DATA Chakra energy Crown,B,C',D',E',F',G',A',B',C'
180 DATA Chakra energy Gr1,_B,_C,_D,_E,_F,_G,A,B,C
190 DATA Chakra energy Third eye,A,B,C',D',E',F',G',A',B'
200 DATA Chakra energy Psychic
center,_A,_B,_C,_D,_E,_F,_G,A,B
210 DATA Chakra energy Gr2,_A,_B,_C,_D,_E,_F,_G,A,B
220 DATA Chakra energy Gr3,^G,^A,^B,^C,^D,^E,^F,^G,^A
230 DATA Chakra energy Throat,G,A,B,C',D',E',F',G',A'
240 DATA Chakra energy
Thymus,^F,^G,^A,^B,^C,^D,^E,^F,^G
250 DATA Chakra energy Heart,F,G,A,B,C',D',E',F',G'
260 DATA Chakra energy Solar
plexus,_E,_F,_G,_A,_B,_C,_D,_E,_F
270 DATA Chakra energy
Diaphragm,^D,^E,^F,^G,^A,^B,^C,^D,^E
280 DATA Chakra energy Gr3,D',E',F',G',A',B',C',D',E'
290 DATA Chakra energy Polarity,D,E,F,G,A,B,C',D',E'
300 DATA Chakra energy Root,C,D,E,F,G,A,B,C',D'
310 DATA Speed of sound
Personality,C',D',E',D',E',F',G',A',B'
320 DATA Speed of sound Circuation and
Sex,^C,^D,^E,^F,^G,^A,^B,^C,^D
330 DATA Speed of sound Adrenals Thyroid
Parathyroid,B,C',D',E',F',G',A',B',C'
340 DATA Speed of sound
Kidneys,_B,_C,_D,_E,_F,_G,A,B,C
350 DATA Speed of sound Liver,_B,_C,_D,_E,_F,_G,A,B,C
360 DATA Speed of sound
Bladder,^F,^G,^A,^B,^C,^D,^E,^F,^G
370 DATA Speed of sound Small
Intestine,^C,^D,^E,^F,^G,^A,^B,^C,^D
380 DATA Speed of sound Lungs,A,B,C',D',E',F',G',A',B'

```
390 DATA Speed of sound Colon,^F,^G,^A,^B,^C,^D,^E,^F,^G
400 DATA Speed of sound Gall Bladder,E,F,G,A,B,C',D',E',F'
410 DATA Speed of sound Pancreas,^C,^D,^E,^F,^G,^A,^B,^C,^D
420 DATA Speed of sound Stomach,A,B,C',D',E',F',G',A',B'
430 DATA Speed of sound Spleen,B,C',D',E',F',G',A',B',C'
440 DATA Speed of sound Blood,_E,_F,_G,_A,_B,_C,_D,_E,_F
450 DATA Speed of sound Fat Cells,^C,^D,^E,^F,^G,^A,^B,^C,^D
460 DATA Speed of sound Muscles,E,F,G,A,B,C',D',E',F'
470 DATA Speed of sound Bone,_A,_B,_C,_D,_E,_F,_G,A,B
480 DATA Mineral Chromium,^G,^A,^B,^C,^D,^E,^F,^G,^A
490 DATA Mineral Molybdenum,F,G,A,B,C',D',E',F',G'
500 DATA Mineral Calcium,E,F,G,A,B,C',D',E',F'
510 DATA Mineral Manganese,^G,^A,^B,^C,^D,^E,^F,^G,^A
520 DATA Mineral Iron,_A,_B,_C,_D,_E,_F,_G,A,B
530 DATA Mineral Potassium,^D,^E,^F,^G,^A,^B,^C,^D,^E
540 DATA Mineral Iodine,_A,_B,_C,_D,_E,_F,_G,A,B
550 DATA Mineral Copper,_B,_C,_D,_E,_F,_G,A,B,C
560 DATA Mineral Phosphorus,B,C',D',E',F',G',A',B',C'
570 DATA Mineral Zinc,B,C',D',E',F',G',A',B',C'
580 DATA Mineral Selenium,^C,^D,^E,^F,^G,^A,^B,^C,^D
590 DATA Planet Spin Earth note,^F,^G,^A,^B,^C,^D,^E,^F,^G
600 DATA Planet Spin Sun note,B,C',D',E',F',G',A',B',C'
610 DATA Planet Spin Moon note,_A,_B,_C,_D,_E,_F,_G,A,B
620 DATA Planet Spin Mars note,G,A,B,C',D',E',F',G',A'
630 DATA Planet Spin Mercury note,A,B,C',D',E',F',G',A',B'
640 DATA Planet Spin Jupiter note,_B,_C,_D,_E,_F,_G,A,B,C
650 DATA Planet Spin Venus note,^G,^A,^B,^C,^D,^E,^F,^G,^A
```

660 DATA Planet Spin Saturn note,^A,^B,^C,^D,^E,^F,^G,^A,^B
670 DATA Planet Spin Uranus note,_A,_B,_C,_D,_E,_F,_G,A,B
680 DATA Planet Spin Neptune note,_E,_F,_G,_A,_B,_C,_D,_E,_F
690 DATA Planet Spin Pluto note,B,C',D',E',F',G',A',B',C'
700 DATA Sine Sounds Personality,^C,^D,^E,^F,^G,^A,^B,^C,^D
710 DATA Sine Sounds Circulation and Sex,^C,^D,^E,^F,^G,^A,^B,^C,^D
720 DATA Sine Sounds Adrenals Thyroid Parathyroid,B,C',D',E',F',G',A',B',C'
730 DATA Sine Sounds Kidney,E,F,G,A,B,C',D',E',F'
740 DATA Sine Sounds Liver,_A,_B,_C,_D,_E,_F,_G,A,B
750 DATA Sine Sounds Bladder,^F,^G,^A,^B,^C,^D,^E,^F,^G
760 DATA Sine Sounds Small Intestine,^C,^D,^E,^F,^G,^A,^B,^C,^D
770 DATA Sine Sounds Lungs,A,B,C',D',E',F',G',A',B'
780 DATA Sine Sounds Colon,^F,^G,^A,^B,^C,^D,^E,^F,^G
790 DATA Sine Sounds Gall Bladder,E,F,G,A,B,C',D',E',F'
800 DATA Sine Sounds Pancreas,^C,^D,^E,^F,^G,^A,^B,^C,^D
810 DATA Sine Sounds Stomach,A,B,C',D',E',F',G',A',B'
820 DATA Sine Sounds Spleen,B,C',D',E',F',G',A',B',C'
830 DATA Chakra Room Root,C,D,E,F,G,A,B,C',D'
840 DATA Chakra Room Polarity,D,E,F,G,A,B,C,D,E
850 DATA Chakra Room Diaphragm,^D,^E,^F,^G,^A,^B,^C,^D,^E
860 DATA Chakra Room Solar Plexus,E,F,G,A,B,C',D',E',F'
870 DATA Chakra Room Heart,F,G,A,B,C',D',E',F',G'
880 DATA Chakra Room Throat,G,A,B,C',D',E',F',G',A'
890 DATA Chakra Room Venusian,^G,^A,^B,^C,^D,^E,^F,^G,^A

900 DATA Chakra Room Gaia
(Earth),^C,^D,^E,^F,^G,^A,^B,^C,^D
910 DATA Chakra Room Psychic
Center,_A,_B,_C,_D,_E,_F,_G,A,B
920 DATA Chakra Room Third
Eye,_B,_C,_D,_E,_F,_G,A,B,C
930 DATA Chakra Room Crown,B,C',D',E',F',G',A',B',C'
940 DATA Chakra Room
Transpersonal,^C,^D,^E,^F,^G,^A,^B,^C,^D
950 DATA Chakra Room
Diaphragm,^D,^E,^F,^G,^A,^B,^C,^D,^E
960 DATA Chakra Room
Polarity,^D,^E,^F,^G,^A,^B,^C,^D,^E
970 DATA Chakra Room Ccrown,B,C',D',E',F',G',A',B',C'
980 DATA Organ Blood,E,F,G,A,B,C',D',E',F'
990 DATA Organ Adrenals,B,C',D',E',F',G',A',B',C'
1000 DATA Organ Kidney,_E,_F,_G,_A,_B,_C,_D,_E,_F
1010 DATA Organ Liver,_E,_F,_G,_A,_B,_C,_D,_E,_F
1020 DATA Organ Bladder,F,G,A,B,C',D',E',F',G'
1030 DATA Organ Intestines,^C,^D,^E,^F,^G,^A,^B,^C,^D
1040 DATA Organ Lungs,A,B,C',D',E',F',G',A',B'
1050 DATA Organ Colon,F,G,A,B,C',D',E',F',G'
1060 DATA Organ Gall Bladder,E,F,G,A,B,C',D',E',F'
1070 DATA Organ Pancreas,^C,^D,^E,^F,^G,^A,^B,^C,^D
1080 DATA Organ Stomach,A,B,C',D',E',F',G',A',B'
1090 DATA Organ Brain,_E,_F,_G,_A,_B,_C,_D,_E,_F
1100 DATA Organ Fat Cells,^C,^D,^E,^F,^G,^A,^B,^C,^D
1110 DATA Organ Muscles,E,F,G,A,B,C',D',E',F'
1120 DATA Organ Bone,_A,_B,_C,_D,_E,_F,_G,A,B
1130 DATA Orbit Earth note,^C,^D,^E,^F,^G,^A,^B,^C,^D
1140 DATA Orbit Sun note,E,F,G,A,B,C',D',E',F'
1150 DATA Orbit Moom note,_A,_B,_C,_D,_E,_F,_G,A,B
1160 DATA Orbit Mars note,D,E,F,G,A,B,C,D,E
1170 DATA Orbit Mercury note,D,E,F,G,A,B,C,D,E

```
1180 DATA Orbit Jupiter note,^F,^G,^A,^B,^C,^D,^E,^F,^G
1190 DATA Orbit Venus note,A,B,C',D',E',F',G',A',B'
1200 DATA Orbit Saturn note,^D,^E,^F,^G,^A,^B,^C,^D,^E
1210 DATA Orbit Uranus note,^G,^A,^B,^C,^D,^E,^F,^G,^A
1220 DATA Orbit Neptune note,_A,_B,_C,_D,_E,_F,_G,A,B
1230 DATA Orbit Pluto note,^C,^D,^E,^F,^G,^A,^B,^C,^D
1240 REM ancient Greek modes
```

ΒΙΒΛΙΟΓΡΑΦΙΑ

Αναφορές για την αρχαιοελληνική απόκρυφη μουσική.

1. Anderson, Warren D. Music and Musicians in Ancient Greece. Cornell Univ. Press, 1994.
2. Aristoxenus, The Harmonics of Aristoxenus, translated by H. S. Macran (Oxford, Barker, Andrew. Greek Musical Writings, 2 vols. Cambridge University Press, 1984 (v.I), 1989 (v.II).
3. Boethius: Fundamentals of Music. (De institutione musica), ed. C. Palisca, trans. C. Bower. Yale 1989.
4. Calrendon, 1902; facs. Hildesheim, G. Olms, 1974).
5. Godwin, Joscelyn. Harmonies of Heaven and Earth: Mysticism in Music from Antiquity to the Avant-Garde. Inner Traditions, 1995.
6. Godwin, Joscelyn. The Harmony of the Spheres: A Sourcebook of the Pythagorean Tradition in Music. Inner Traditions, 1993.
7. Godwin, Joscelyn. Music, Mysticism and Magic: A Sourcebook. Arkana, 1986.
8. Godwin, Joscelyn. The Mystery of the Seven Vowels. Phanes, 1991.
9. Nicomachus. The Manual of Harmonics of Nicomachus the Pythagorean, transl. & commentary by Flora R. Levin. Phanes, 1994. Also translated by Barker (vol. II, ch. 10).
10. Henderson, Isobel (1957). Ancient Greek Music in The New Oxford History of Music,

vol.1: Ancient and Oriental Music, Oxford, Oxford University Press.

11. Plato. Laws, (700-701a).
12. Plato. Republic, (398d-399a).
13. Pole, William. The Philosophy of Music, 6th ed. Kegan Paul, Trench, Trubner & Co., 1924.
14. Virgil, The Aeneid (trans. John Dryden).
15. Wellesz, Egon. "Music in the Treatises of Greek Gnostics and Alchemists," pp. 145-58.
16. Werner, Eric. "The Origin of the Eight Modes of Music (Octoechos)," Hebrew Union College Annual, Vol. XXI (1948), pp. 211-55.
17. Williams, C.F. (1903). The Story of the Organ, New York: Charles Scribner and Sons.
18. Winnington-Ingram, R. P. Mode in Ancient Greek Music. Adolf M. Hakkert, 1968.
19. Zorzos Gregory, many-many books about logodynamics, Createspace-Amazon.

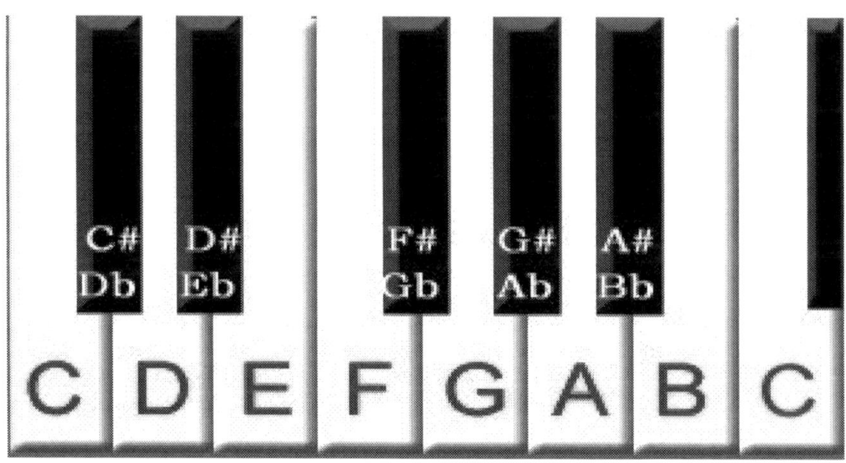

Made in the USA
Columbia, SC
09 February 2020

87701143R00138